Christianity and the New Spirit of Capitalism

Christianity and the New Spirit of Capitalism

KATHRYN TANNER

Yale UNIVERSITY PRESS

New Haven and London

Published with assistance from the foundation established
in memory of James Wesley Cooper of the Class of 1865,
Yale College.

Yale University Press books may be purchased in quantity for
educational, business, or promotional use. For information, please
e-mail sales.press@yale.edu (U.S. office) or sales@yaleup.co.uk
(U.K. office).

Set in Minion type by IDS Infotech Ltd.
Printed in the United States of America.

Library of Congress Control Number: 2018939346

ISBN 978-0-300-21903-6 (hardcover : alk. paper)

A catalogue record for this book is available from the British
Library.

This paper meets the requirements of ANSI/NISO Z39.48-1992
(Permanence of Paper).

10 9 8 7 6 5 4 3 2 1

For Linn Marie Tonstad

Be the evils what they may, the experiment is not yet played out.

—ISABELLE STENGERS

Contents

Acknowledgments

This book began with a Henry Luce III Fellowship in 2010, and the research and writing continued for seven years until I delivered the Gifford Lectures at the University of Edinburgh in spring 2017. I am very grateful to David and Margot Fergusson for their hospitality during my stay.

I wish to thank the following people for their friendship in the difficult time between the start and finish of this book: Catherine Keller, Virginia Burrus, Saul Olyan, Joy McDougall, Laurel Schneider and Emilie Townes, Bill Schweiker, Serene Jones, David Newheiser and Alda Balthrop-Lewis, Miroslav Volf, Dale Martin, my neighbors on Shore Drive, Beryl Satter, and all the very kind students and colleagues who have made up the community of Yale Divinity School during those years. Three very special people did their best to shepherd me along: Teresa Berger, Jackie Winter, and most especially Linn Marie Tonstad to whom this book is dedicated.

Many people read and commented on the manuscript or portions of it, among them Yale Divinity School masters students in a course on work and debt, doctoral students and faculty in the areas of theology, philosophy of religion, and ethics at Yale University (in particular Ryan Darr, Jennifer Herdt,

and John Hare), Chuck Mathewes, Karen Kilby, David Newheiser, Daniel Schultz, Patrick Brennan, Russell Keat, Andrew
Prevot, Ted Smith, and the readers for Yale University Press,
John Thiel, and Ian McFarland. I also benefited mightily from
the expert guidance of my editor at Yale University Press, Jennifer Banks. Rona Johnson Gordon did me the invaluable
service of helping to cut an overly long last chapter at the elev-
enth hour.

All have done their part to remind me that God's grace
can come through intelligent, good, and highly competent
people; for that I am deeply grateful.

Christianity and the New Spirit of Capitalism

1

The New Spirit of Capitalism and a Christian Response

The title of this book calls to mind Max Weber's *Protestant Ethic and the Spirit of Capitalism*.[1] Weber discusses how Christian commitments were formative of capitalism at its start. Indeed, he comes close to suggesting that certain Christian beliefs (or others with functionally equivalent effects on economic behavior) were *necessary* to get capitalism started, given the oddity of what capitalism demanded of people: working more than was necessary to meet basic needs.

Weber wonders where a capitalist form of economic organization found people willing to act in the way it required, particularly at capitalism's start, when there were other ways to make a living—when, for example, one could support oneself in the style to which one was accustomed through subsistence farming, through barter or simple trade, and so on. There is, according to Weber, nothing self-evident, nothing commonplace, about what capitalism asks from people. Proving that lack of self-evidence is capitalism's penchant for destroying the traditional ways of living that precede it.

Indeed, part of Weber's project is to make capitalism seem unnatural, writing as he does in the already industrialized West, in which the reasonableness of capitalism could easily be taken for granted. Only by problematizing capitalism—turning it into a problem for sustained consideration of its existence and value—is he able to show the need for the sort of sociological explanation he offers for it.

Thus, capitalism is oddly aimless in human terms in that its "deliberate, and systematic adjustment of economic means to the [end of] profit" seems freed, Weber believes, from any limits established by need.[2] Capitalism, at least in its startup phase, detaches, in other words, the pursuit of profit from the end of happiness, and in that way comes to make money an end in itself and to counsel hard work for its own sake. No matter how much money one makes, one is never satisfied. Material needs may be met but that does not still the pursuit of more money; one always wants more of it, whatever one's achieved state of happiness. Indeed, one is willing to defer the enjoyment of life—perhaps indefinitely—in favor of the hard work necessary to make more money.

For all the careful means/ends, and in that sense rational, calculation typical of capitalism, there is something unnatural, even irrational, about all this when considered from the standpoint of the satisfaction of basic material needs—if, that is, one's end is simply to live well according to established standards of the times, as Weber thinks was the case before capitalism got up and running in the West. According to Weber: "Under capitalism, [humans] are dominated by the making of money, by acquisition as the ultimate purpose of life. Economic acquisition is no longer subordinated to [the human] as the means for the satisfaction of material needs. This reversal of what we should call the natural relationship, so irrational from a naïve point of view, is evidently as definitely a leading principle of capitalism as it is foreign to all peoples not under capitalistic influence."[3]

Weber argues that people are initially motivated to act in these otherwise inexplicable ways for religious reasons; religious motives lie behind the appeal of capitalism at its start and explain the willingness of people to take it up as a going concern when they have other options. Thus, hard work in the pursuit of profit comes to take precedence over the pursuit of happiness when such conduct is taken to be a sign of one's ultimate destiny, of being among those favored by God for salvation after death. Hard work in the pursuit of profit serves no particular material ends, and in that way becomes an end in itself considered in this-worldly terms, because of its primary significance for an otherworldly end: salvation.[4]

More specifically, a religiously inspired psychological sanction for hard work in the pursuit of profit reaches its height, Weber thinks, among religious people of a Calvinist stripe who believe in double predestination—that God predestines for all eternity some to salvation and some to damnation—and where the only effective way of stilling anxiety about whether one is saved or damned is the outwardly disciplined character of one's everyday behavior without regard for material enjoyment. *If* one is graced by God, among the elect, one's ordinary pursuits will be coolly self-disciplined, restrained, non-hedonistic, and in that way amenable to capitalist requirements as a kind of unintended consequence.

Weber thinks the duty, the obligation of hard work remains, even when the religious beliefs that support it drop away, as he thought they had in his day, in the heyday of industrial capitalism at the turn of the twentieth century. Without knowing exactly why, other than it has become a necessary part of his life, "[the business man] exists for the sake of his business, rather than the reverse."[5] He gets nothing out of his wealth except "the irrational sense of having done his job well."[6] Once it becomes a going concern, capitalism itself educates people to feel this way, it habituates people into this sort of ethic, and it therefore no longer matters whether they are religious or not. Indeed, the specifically religious underpinnings of such a work ethic, while continuing to haunt it, can easily become an unnecessary, even unproductive, distraction from values now directly attached to the work itself.

The present book shares with Weber the idea that religious beliefs (Christian beliefs specifically) have the capacity to provide powerful psychological sanctions for economic behavior, whether intentionally or not. However controversial Weber's specific thesis about the significance of Calvinism for the genesis of capitalism in the West is—and I have no interest in disputing the criticisms made of that thesis over the years—Weber might still be right about religion's practical efficacy, its ability to shape believers' conduct in everyday life, and in that way have a bearing on their economic behavior.

Of primary importance for that determination is not the explicit ethical teachings of Christianity about economic matters but what Weber calls "practical impulses for action, founded in psychological and pragmatic contexts of religion."[7] It is never apparent from those ethical teachings alone the degree to which they are taken seriously and acted upon. Such teachings are indeed practically irrelevant if there are no effective psychological sanctions for recommended actions that come by way of specifically religious interests, most powerfully those pertaining to salvation—how to gain it and how to be sure of it. Religious interests motivate action, get people to act; religious ideas specify the character of those interests and the directions by which they might be satisfied—they are the switchmen, Weber says, determining the tracks along which action is pushed by religious interests.[8] In his words,

> We are naturally not concerned with the question of what was theoretically and officially taught in the ethical compendia of the time, however much practical significance this may have had through the influence of Church discipline, pastoral work, and preaching. We are interested rather in something entirely different: the influence of those psychological sanctions which, originating in religious belief and the practice of religion, gave a direction to practical conduct and held the individual to it. Now these sanctions were to a large extent derived from the peculiarities of the religious ideas behind them. [People] of that day were occupied with abstract dogmas to an extent which can only be understood when we perceive the connections of those dogmas with practical religious interests.[9]

To restate this Weberian approach in my own terms, religious beliefs, whether of obviously practical import or not, are meant not just to be believed but to be lived, to orient behavior, attitudes, and actions toward oneself and others. Those beliefs motivate action by establishing the value of certain states of affairs (salvation) and by telling people either how to get there, their means of access to them, or at least how to prove or test one's being in them (often in both cases, for example, by the doing of good deeds). Religious beliefs also effectively steer action by making only certain courses of action seem reasonable. For example, if the world is about to end in fire, it might make better sense to retire to a bunker in Idaho than run for Congress. What one believes about the world establishes in great part what it makes sense to do.[10]

Signally important here are not simply the logical consequences of religious beliefs but their psychological impacts. The logical consequence of predestination is, one might argue with Weber, a resigned fatalism: it does not matter what one does, since one's destiny, whether for good or ill, is predetermined by God and therefore taken out of one's own hands. But the psychological effect of double predestination, as Weber believes the historical record shows, is anxiety about one's fate, an anxiety that comes to be stilled, it turns out, only by signs running contrary to what the doctrine logically implies. The very rejection of fatalism, through active commitment to one's own self-improvement, becomes proof of election.[11]

Where religious interests and their pursuit are not cordoned off from everyday life but attribute considerable importance to what happens there—where, for example, religious vocations are not confined to specifically religious institutions (such as monasteries)—Christian beliefs, by all the mechanisms noted, might form life conduct generally, permeate life in all respects so as to establish a whole way of living, with significant economic impacts.

This book shares much of Weber's methodology then—a methodology that is humanistic in its concern for the practical efficacy of religious beliefs. Whatever those beliefs' sources—whether stemming from a purported special revelation or from rational investigation of the natural world—at issue is their consequences for human life, a matter of general human, and not simply religious, concern.

My aim as a theologian in using such a method, however, is the opposite of Weber's. Contrary to his project, I hope to show how Christian beliefs (a specific variant of them that is perhaps equally odd but arguably as historically widespread as puritanical Calvinism) might *undermine* rather than support the *new* spirit of capitalism.

What Christianity gives it can also take away; the behaviors that Christian beliefs suborn may easily align with capitalism's demands or be in significant tension with them. What matters, as Weber well knew, is the specific character of those beliefs in practical application. Not every stripe of Christian belief could provide a religiously inspired sanction for conduct of the sort Weber thought typical of capitalism at its start. Backed up by whatever empirical correlations he thought he could find between capitalist and Calvinist commitment, Weber spent a great deal of time comparing and contrasting the possible practical ramifications of variations in basic religious outlooks. Whether amenable to capitalism at its start or not, my own Christian commitments as I hope to show are inimical to the demands of capitalism now.

I am critical of the present spirit of capitalism because I believe my own, quite specific Christian commitments require it. But I also suggest over the course of the chapters to come that the present-day organization of capitalism is deserving of such criticism whatever one's religious commitments, because of its untoward effects on persons and populations, its deforming effects on the way people understand themselves and their relations with others. Every way of organizing economic life is flawed. Besides having especially egregious faults (relative to other ways that capitalism has been organized, this one foments, for example, extreme income/wealth inequality, structural under- and unemployment, and regularly recurring boom/bust cycles in asset values), what is unusual about the present system is the way its spirit hampers recognition of those faults. The present-day spirit of capitalism needs to be undermined, therefore, in order for the current system to be problematized—seen as a problem amenable to solution, an object of possible criticism requiring redress. And in order for that to happen, in order for the spirit of present-day capitalism to be effectively undermined, it needs to be met, I suggest, by a counter-spirit of similar power. Without the need any longer of religious backing, capitalism may now have the power itself to shape people in its own image; its conduct-forming spirit may now be its own production, in other words. But as one of the few alternative outlooks on life with a capacity to shape life conduct to a comparable degree, religion might remain a critical force against it.

Modern philosophy, for example, has reneged on its character as a spirituality, in Michel Foucault's sense (following Pierre Hadot); it has lost the earlier capacity it had in Stoicism or Cynicism to bring along with it a person-shaping way of life to be laid at the feet of capitalism as either its rival or companion.[12] While certainly not recommending some repristination of earlier forms of spirituality, Foucault himself clearly thought those earlier non-Christian spiritualities suggested the possibility of more free-spirited experiments in ways of living, social experiments that might effectively resist contemporary capitalism by redirecting the very means of controlling conduct promoted by it—that is, by way of the neoliberal capitalist demand itself for self-realizing, entrepreneurial subjects. Whether Foucault is right or not about the way pastoral power in Christianity funded current regimes of governmentality—whether Weber is right or not about Protestantism's support for a capitalist work ethic—I attempt to show in this book how other, historically significant strands of Christianity with which I identify hold out the better hope of effective resistance when compared, for example, with the various types of non-Christian spirituality explored by Foucault. These Christian beliefs work at the same nodal point for the contemporary conducting of conduct that Foucault identifies—ethical self-formation—but with far more radically transformative effects, with far greater capacity for contrast with what contemporary capitalism demands of people in the effort to align their behavior with its own mechanisms for profit generation.

Finance-Dominated Capitalism

The capitalism of today is finance-dominated (as well as finance-disciplined), and as such it has its own distinctive spirit, by which I mean much the same thing as Weber did: cultural forms—beliefs, values, and norms—that accompany capitalism to help shape subjects and social relations more generally to meet its requirements.

Whatever the specific organizational shapes it assumes, capitalism always brings along with it, as part of its normal functioning, cultural forms affecting how subjects relate to themselves and to others. Capitalism has cultural concomitants—beliefs, values, and norms—that direct conduct, that get people to do willingly what capitalism requires of them by encouraging them to see what they are doing—what they *must* do to get ahead—as meaningful, valuable, or simply inevitable.[13]

More than just supplying an after the fact justification—by suggesting, for example, their moral legitimacy—such cultural concomitants of capitalism amount to practical directives, helping to elicit and orient the very behaviors that capitalism mandates. Thus, while I may believe that acting in a cutthroat way for my own personal benefit is ultimately for the good of all and therefore morally legitimate, what actually brings me to act that way is the belief, encouraged by an unrelentingly competitive economic environment, that if I do not look out for myself no one else will. Cultural forms of the latter sort, ones that directly govern conduct, constitute the spirit of capitalism in the sense to be developed here.[14]

As Weber recognized, the spirit of capitalism (like capitalism itself considered simply as an economic organization) is constituted at any one time by a historically specific constellation of forces and influences (rather than being the simple instantiation of some general, ahistorical class).[15] There are, then, potentially multiple spirits of capitalism across (and I would also say, for much the same reasons, within each one of) the mutating arrangements that make up capitalism in virtue of such historically variable conjunctions.[16] The spirit of capitalism today is not the same as the spirit Weber discusses (nor, as we shall see, is it identical with the utilitarian spirit he thought was coming to replace it in his own day).

In the remainder of this chapter let me discuss a bit more what I mean by finance-dominated capitalism and outline its specific spirit, before offering a précis of what is to come. Here and in succeeding chapters, my account of this form of capitalism and its spirit are offered as ideal types in a Weberian sense of that phrase: that is, they are analytical constructs that accentuate certain aspects of the messy realities of the current economic and cultural scene and show how they might be brought together into relationships with an internal consistency.[17] While not necessarily logically consistent, the elements I highlight prove mutually reinforcing, for example, in service of the same practical end of maximizing profit. As ideal types, they should not be confused with reality: No actual corporation or state government is likely to be run in complete conformity with the dictates of finance as I describe them. As ideal types they are designed for heuristic purposes—to bring greater clarity to the understanding and evaluation of what are admittedly irreducibly singular cases.

Contemporary capitalism is finance dominated in several senses. First, simply, finance-generated profit has growing importance for contemporary capitalism. Profit in the financial sector (for example, banking, insurance, real estate) is a growing percentage of national income when compared with the industrial or service sectors. Profit from financial dealings is also of increasing significance to nonfinancial firms. For example, car companies routinely make more money from loaning money to buy cars than from selling them. According to one scholar, "General Electric (GE), Sears, General Motors, Ford . . . all created captive finance units that were originally intended to support consumer purchases of their products by offering installment financing but which eventually became financial behemoths that overshadowed the manufacturing or retailing activities of the parent firm."[18] Contemporary capitalism is marked furthermore by increased financial activity. That is, the amount of money and frequency of transactions in finance dwarf that of other economic activities. It is not uncommon, for instance, for the money changing hands on foreign currency exchanges in a single day to equal that of the whole of world trade in a year.

This shift to finance is no doubt propelled by the oversized profits to be made there, when compared with industrial production or the nonfinancial service sector. While clearly aided by tax policy and reserve requirements for investment banking, financial dealings are in principle far more profitable than other ways of making money; one can literally triple one's money overnight. This is partly a function of volatility in financial markets: the prices of assets on financial markets typically rise (and fall) quite sharply and rapidly (for reasons that are discussed in a moment). But it is also a result of the common use of leverage in financial dealings, that is, the use of borrowed money to make them. If I buy a stock with my own money for $100 and the price of that stock goes up by $1 the next day, my rate of return is obviously far smaller than if I had initially borrowed $99 to buy it. If I bought the stock with my own money, I had $100 and now I have $101, for a measly 1 percent return. But if I borrowed $99 of the purchase price, I would have doubled my own money (minus whatever interest and principal were paid on the loan of $99 in the meantime); I had $1 and now I have $2.

This comparatively greater rate of return in finance often figures in reasons given for the initial shift to a finance-dominated form of capitalism. For a variety of reasons—depending on the economist one asks—the rate of profit by other means—say, industrial production—tends eventually to fall, or simply historically did fall for exogenous reasons, beginning in the 1970s. The exogenous culprit might be increased competition from overseas, along with wage inflexibility brought about by strong unions. Changes simply in the composition of capital in production (for example, more capital sunk in equipment or in technological advances permitting greater productivity with fewer workers) and/or a fall-off in demand relative to productive capacity might also be to blame. Whatever the exact reason, at a certain point since the 1970s there has been nowhere for profits from production of goods and services to be invested profitably aside from finance; finance is the only place where big money can still be made.[19]

In order to be an easy remedy for a declining rate of profit elsewhere and not be dragged down by the very same forces of stagnation or slow growth, finance needs to bypass any direct link with the production of goods and services. This is the second sense in which capitalism is finance dominated: finance is no longer directly in service of production elsewhere but takes on a life of its own, so to speak. Finance remains of course a helpful, even necessary aid to nonfinancial industrial and service sectors. For example, a company (especially when just starting up and therefore without capital accruing from profits) might need a loan to purchase equipment or a retailer, to stock shelves, with the money to pay back these loans coming from profits made through the actual sale of goods and services. A declining rate of profit from such sales would presumably hurt profits from finance too—businesses might have difficulty paying back these loans, the demand for them might fall, and so on.

Loans for consumption purposes—credit card loans, payday loans, home equity loans—are one way of making finance's dependence on profit from sale of goods and services less direct. In a stagnating economy demand for such loans as a supplement or replacement for wages only goes up rather than down. Presumably if businesses are having trouble paying back their loans, consumers would be having trouble too since wages typically used to pay off such loans are also ultimately dependent on corporate profits. But consumers can be squeezed in ways that less flexible corporations often cannot be. Short of "ceasing operations"—which in the individual consumer's case means losing one's capacity to live—consumers often can—and denied the same generous bankruptcy protections afforded corporations, often must—cut back to the bone their other expenditures in order to service a debt. When consumer loan terms are not so onerous as to sap the consumption they are purportedly for the sake of, such loans could also presumably help to resolve any profitability problem with loans to corporations for production purposes. Consumer loans, by fueling demand, might help make the production of goods and services more profitable, thereby indirectly supporting the profitability of loans for such purposes.

But better yet, as a way to avoid being dragged down by stagnation in the industrial and service sectors, is profit generated through the trading of financial instruments themselves, that is, the creation of secondary markets where loans, stocks, and so on are themselves subject to sale. Such secondary markets (in principle) make for instant liquidity: one does not have to hold onto a financial instrument but can sell it to someone else at any time (unless of course every other market participant wants to sell at the same time and there is no one left to buy). Stock markets are the most familiar form of secondary market for financial instruments, but secondary markets now exist for just about anything with a claim on future revenue. Mortgages, for example, are almost always immediately sold, enabling the initiating party to unload the risks of default and of declining returns through interest rate hikes or inflation, and providing through their very sale a source of capital for new mortgages (rather than through old-fashioned commercial bank deposits.) This is one way that finance frees itself from being dependent on and therefore adversely affected by an otherwise stagnating economy: "finance mostly finances finance."[20]

The way prices are set by secondary markets has the same finance-financing-finance effect, freeing profits generated there from being limited by tepid growth and low employment in the rest of the economy. While prices of a company's stock are no doubt influenced by current and likely future profitability of that company, they are directly set by current and expected demand for the stock on a stock exchange, which need not be at all proportionate to the former. Demand for stocks generally might be heavily influenced, for example, by institutional investors such as pension funds, by tax policy favoring capital gains, and so on—by anything that affects the volume of purchases on the stock market. A shift to finance as the privileged site for profit generation arguably leads itself to inflation of the value of financial assets such as stocks. But more specifically, the value of any one stock tends to become uncoupled from underlying fundamentals just to the degree that expectations about the behavior of other investors are what is fueling demand for it. If one bought a stock with the expectation of making money through the distribution of dividends from company profits over the long term, the profitability of the company should reasonably be the basis for one's decision to buy it. If one buys a stock in order to sell it for a higher price sometime later, increased demand for it at that later moment of sale is all one is reasonably counting on in purchasing it. The effect of every investor doing this is captured nicely (albeit somewhat unfortunately) by John Maynard Keynes's analogy of the beauty contest.[21] Picking the most beautiful contestant, based on one's assessment of her (or his) loveliness, is not at issue; instead one is trying to predict the contestant that most of the other judges will pick, with every one of the judges, as well as oneself, trying to do the same thing. Opinion simply chases opinion then, with the likely effect of a self-fulfilling prophecy decoupled from objective attributes. To return to the stock market, expectation of greater demand for a stock—perhaps prompted by some good news about profits that quarter—itself fuels greater demand for the stock; the price of the stock goes up accordingly—perhaps way up depending on the number of people convinced that other people hold such a favorable opinion of the stock—thereby confirming the expectation of a price rise and fueling even greater demand. The value of financial assets on secondary markets can for these reasons shoot up (and down) rather wildly from day to day in ways that simply do not reflect any comparably dramatic changes in, for example, a corporation's bottom line.

But the mass of new financial products that repackage financial instruments—derivatives—and the secondary markets for them are perhaps the means by which finance-generated profits become most indirectly related to the production of goods and services, often nearly decoupled from it.[22] Derivatives are commonly defined as financial instruments whose value is indexed to other financial instruments. Derivatives often serve the purpose of hedging against risks stemming from movements in the value of currencies, and therefore interest rates, with the demise of the Bretton Woods agreements that pegged all national currencies to the dollar backed by gold. This purpose has been frequently proffered as a reason for their multiplication. Some of these risks have the potential to adversely impact the bottom line of nonfinancial corporations, and therefore to this extent such financial products would remain in service of the production of goods and services. For example, because of international outsourcing and transnational operations and sales, the profitability of corporations is increasingly affected by currency exchange-rate fluctuations; derivatives provide a way of limiting exposure to such risks, of limiting the damages when, because of such fluctuations, the costs of the inputs one buys overseas balloon, while the prices for the goods one is trying to sell on other foreign markets become uncompetitive, that is, too expensive for people there to be willing to buy. One gains such protection by in effect betting against oneself: one buys a derivative that will provide a pay-out to your company in the very circumstances that would otherwise hurt it.

Credit default swaps—those most toxic of assets in the recent financial crisis—provide another example of derivatives functioning as insurance; in the subprime mortgage crisis they were a (failed) form of insurance policy against the loss in value of the mortgages that formed the basis for another sort of derivative, collateralized debt obligations (CDOs). If one owned such a CDO and were concerned about its possible decline in value, one could insure against that through a credit default swap whereby a second party would assume the risk, by guaranteeing the value of the CDO in case of default in the underlying mortgages.

The CDOs insured against here, like a great many other forms of derivatives, are clearly designed to be profit generating in themselves, apart from any benefit provided to nonfinancial corporations. CDOs repackaged mortgages, especially subprime mortgages with high-interest payments attractive to investors looking for higher than normal yields, into bonds made up of separate tranches or slices of those underlying mortgages, the varying interest rates of such tranches being determined by investors' willingness to assume risk: investors in the higher interest tranches would be paid back last in the case of default. It is the repackaging here, along with the existence of secondary markets for what has been repackaged—and the capacity for what has already been repackaged once to be repackaged again in turn, without any apparent limit (CDOs squared)—that is itself profit generating, in ways that are therefore set loose from sagging profits through production. For CDOs to be profitable one does not need a million new houses to be built in an otherwise booming economy (although that might help): one simply needs the existing houses to recirculate, or, short of that, the people currently owning houses to refinance. Simple circulation—repackaging, reselling—of financial instruments in the case of derivatives means that in this situation M-M—money directly produces more money—rather than M-C-M—money by way of the sale of other commodities—holds.

But even where derivatives serve useful insurance functions they are commonly decoupled from the sort of ownership interests that are of help to nonfinancial corporations; they become simple bets on the part of otherwise disinterested parties. Corporations buy derivatives because they have an ownership interest in products and services denominated in different currencies, that is, because of what they otherwise buy (say, equipment) and sell (their company outputs). But as the volume of the market in them suggests, derivatives with insurance functions are purchased to be profitable in their own right, independent of any ownership interests in what underlies them. They become in effect like insurance policies taken out on other people's lives and property rather than one's own. Whether one was willing to buy or to sell a credit default swap on a certain CDO or a pool of them, and at what price, became simply a way of betting on the likelihood of widespread subprime mortgage default. Those betting rightly—for example, investors betting on the collapse of the market in credit default swaps and in the CDOs they indexed—could come out ahead even as the economy otherwise crumbled.

Indeed betting is a common feature of derivatives, accounting for the decoupling of profit there from the rest of the economy. Derivatives that involve arbitrage, profit generation by way of disparities in the value of similar assets across different markets, are a prime case in point. One can take advantage of a difference in interest rates among different currencies, for example, by taking out low-interest loans in one currency to fund the sale of higher-interest loans in another. Derivatives like this become in effect nothing more than a bet on the spread, or relative disparity, between different asset values.

The sort of decoupling I have been describing brings with it unusual effects if compared with industrial capitalism or a service economy, that is, with capitalism geared to the production of goods and services. Unlike finance-dominated capitalism, the latter is demand dependent—there have to be people around with the money to buy those goods and services—and therefore capitalism of those sorts cannot make do with an immiserated workforce or massive unemployment. Finance-dominated capitalism is not similarly dependent. Enormous profits can be made in finance in the midst of a deep recession or depression. For example, the lower the general wage level, the more people will be forced into debt in order to make ends meet, the more valuable those loans will be to them, and the more they will be willing to pay for them. Or, in keeping with the example previously noted, one can simply bet on economic decline by, say, shorting stocks or CDOs on secondary markets.

This sort of decoupling of finance from the production of goods and services does not mean, however, that finance and such production go their separate ways. Finance rather comes to discipline all other forms of economic activity—corporate, state, and individual economic activity—and this is the third sense in which contemporary capitalism is finance dominated.

Finance disciplines corporations through corporate efforts to bolster shareholder value.[23] That is, the point of corporate management is to return value to the owners of the corporation, understood as the holders of its stock. The sphere of corporate responsibility—comprising those parties to whom a corporation is responsive and accountable—is restricted to these owners of its stock and includes neither employees (unless they are also stockholders) nor the community in which the corporation is located. Corporations are to be run with the primary intent of simply increasing the value of their shares on the stock exchange.

What such discipline means in practice is a relentless drive toward maximum profitability—not just earnings sufficient to pay one's workers and overhead costs with enough left over to ensure necessary future investment in equipment and some charitable outreach to the community (typified by previous owner-managed small businesses), but maximally efficient use of as few workers as possible with minimal unnecessary expenditures. And this maximum profitability needs to be demonstrated quarterly (that is, continually, in as short a timeframe as possible for nonfinancial institutions that require extended time to produce and sell things), in order to influence the stock market where stock values are being constantly reassessed. In short, discipline by finance—in this case, the stock market—means downsizing, working the employees one retains that much harder to ensure their maximum productivity, outsourcing and shifting operations to lower cost sites regardless of community fallout, and doing all this in ideally rapid sync with changing market conditions, without the time or space to look very far down the road.

This is specifically a market form of discipline (and not simply corporate self-disciplining that happens to align with market imperatives) in that many such management strategies are simply not conducive to the long-term health of corporations. For example, rapid turnover of employees, along with management refusal to engage in long-term planning where it might bring temporary declines in profitability, are likely to be corrosive of corporate profitability over the long haul. But that does not really matter if the financial profits from such management strategies are taking precedence over (nonfinancial) corporate profits. One can cash out one's stock, which (for secondary market demand reasons) has increased in value far more than quarterly profits might warrant, before any damage done to the future profitability of the corporation becomes clear. CEOs paid in unrestricted stock options apparently do this all the time before leaving to be hired elsewhere.

One of the primary mechanisms for enforcing shareholder value also helps make clear that this is a specifically financial market discipline at potential loggerheads with corporate interests: fear of hostile takeover. Whether they like it or not, companies have to be managed to keep their stock values high; if the total stock value of a corporation were to fall below the value of its assets, it might easily be bought up with the intent of simply stripping those company assets—for example, with the intent of selling its real estate holdings and equipment out from under it. In a hostile takeover, moreover, a controlling interest in a company's stock is often gained by borrowing money for purchase of that stock using the company to be acquired as collateral (that is, by issuing corporate junk bonds, whose purchase are themselves lubricated by the creation of secondary markets for them). These loans then go on the company's own books once it is acquired, putting immediate pressure on the profitability of the company by adding to its costs. In addition to its other expenses, the company now needs to pay off the debt to junk bond investors, which means instituting all those cost saving measures that, besides coming at the expense of workers and the wider community, might ultimately do even more harm to the company's bottom line. Aside from money made by investors in the junk bonds (at the company's expense), the financial interests of the now private company's owners are also served: they can take the company public again by selling shares at the inflated prices supposedly warranted by the greater efficiencies that come by way of corporate layoffs.[24]

National, state, and municipal governments are also increasingly disciplined by bondholders, to similar effect. Especially since the 1970s when many burgeoning welfare states faced crippling economic stagnation, nation-states have been unable (or unwilling) to fully fund government operations through taxation. One very significant reason is their desire to attract mobile corporations through lower corporate tax rates; every country (and subsidiary government) tries the same thing, prompting a race to the bottom in those tax rates. Nations turn to private investors to make up the tax revenue shortfall by issuing public debt, such as Treasury bonds and bills in the case of the United States. Servicing those debts increases government costs and forces cost-cutting or austerity measures elsewhere, in much the same way debt servicing works in corporate takeovers using borrowed funds. Cost-cutting means decreasing the size of government, that is, firing employees, working them harder to increase productivity, refusing to use any revenue surpluses to increase wages or workers employed, and so on. But unlike the case with corporations, lowering costs of government also means lowering output: cutting service provision, which, unlike the products and services of corporations, amount to a cost rather than a source of revenue for governments. The state might decrease its funding of infrastructure and education. It might in general renege on previously accepted obligations to guarantee the welfare of the population, through medical or unemployment benefits, for instance. Some of its usual welfare-, education-, and infrastructure-oriented operations can be handed over to private companies, on the assumption that greater efficiencies are likely there (given the fact, for example, that employees of private firms are less likely to be unionized). But many of the tasks and risks that governments used to take direct responsibility for managing can simply be made the responsibility of individuals; individuals must now assume the costs.

The need to attract private investors for funding of government operations at the least possible expense promotes the same sort of disciplining of government policy; the same government policies are put in place not just when pressured by debt servicing but simply as a way of keeping creditors happy and interest on government debt low. Nation-states are credit worthy only if their other expenditures—costs of operation and service provision—are low, making it more likely that they will have the funds to service their debt. One might think, to the contrary, that government policy encouraging economic growth—for example, government investment in education, in roads and bridges, and government efforts to keep interest rates low to encourage corporate investment in equipment—would attract investors to one's bonds; a healthy economy brings with it greater tax revenues, and those might also be expected to increase the likelihood that funds will be available to pay back government debt. But a number of these government measures would cut into the profit of investors in government bonds: low interest rates, for example. And their overall intended effect—a hot economy at full employment—might be similarly damaging to bondholders. That type of economy brings inflation with it, and inflation decreases the value of the interest paid out to bondholders over time. Policies to promote economic growth are therefore understood to make a state less rather than more credit worthy; investors are therefore less likely to want to purchase that state's bonds and will demand a higher rate of return on them. In short, especially in times of recession and high unemployment, when tax revenues fall quite short of expectations, government policy can easily be taken hostage by foreign investors and the increasingly few rich among its own citizens with the ability to make significant purchases of government bonds. Government policy is disciplined against, in other words, the interests of the majority of its citizens. And this is a self-sustaining spiral; the more that government policies to placate bondholders encourage further economic decline, the more dependent government operations become on the rich within and (especially given the amount of money involved) without that state's borders, with the responsiveness and responsibilities of government narrowed to a growing few with interests contrary to those of its own population as a whole.[25]

The disciplining of corporations and governments by finance has the effect of disciplining individuals. Those employed by such corporations and governments are worked harder and live in fear for their jobs. Those laid off by such organizations face the discipline of economic hardship made harder by a state reneging on its previous dedication to the well-being of its people. Out of work or underemployed by finance-disciplined corporations and governments, and without sufficient alternative sources of aid to ease their impoverishment, they may be forced to take out loans to sustain themselves—payday loans, credit card debt, secondhand car loans to make up for lack of public transportation, and so on—thereby coming under direct disciplining by debt themselves.

Indeed, attempts to direct the conduct of individuals become increasingly important in both finance-disciplined corporations and nation-states. For example, maximizing profit through efficiency measures, whether in private corporations or government offices, means getting the most out of every worker. Those efficiency measures target individual workers (rather than groups of workers identified, say, by job description)—for example, by constantly evaluating performance not just against shared team benchmarks but against the performance of every other worker assigned to the same task. Lowering the costs of directing them, both corporations and nation-states increasingly demand of individuals that they become self-managing in line with corporate and state interests; they are to direct themselves and assume responsibility for their own lives, whether at work or outside it, thereby saving both corporation and state the efforts that would otherwise have to be expended to get them to toe the line, to be, for example, healthy and productive workers. Individuals in this way become a target of interest not only in their economic activity but in their lives as a whole. It becomes increasingly difficult to distinguish the character of conduct at work from that outside of it. One must be self-managing of one's assets in an attempt to maximize performance not just at work but in the effort to lead a happy, healthy life. Or, thanks to one's indebtedness, the careful calculation of costs necessary for work efficiency is extended to one's patterns of consumption—one has to count every penny in every arena of life if one is not just to survive but to service one's debt. Contrary to the welfare state's concern for the well-being of the population as a whole (in which individuals are considered under the guise of simple statistical averages), and contrary to a liberal state agenda of laissez-faire, where state action is to be limited to allow for the free operation of individuals in civil society and economic relations, the state here becomes the active arm of international finance, managing society to ensure competitive relations among individual units viewed as independent enterprises, each dedicated to the maximally profitable use of his or her capacities.[26]

The Spirit of Finance-Dominated Capitalism

This discipline (of varying sorts) brings with it a general spirit, a general ethic, for all its specific differences of operation. Max Weber maintains that capitalism would lose the need for any spirit generated independently of it—by religion—once it was up and running. Capitalism, in his famous words, would become an iron cage. Once capitalism became the only game in town, people would be forced to adapt to its behavioral dictates, whether they liked it or not; they would have to conform to a capitalist manner of organizing economic behavior or starve. "At present," says Weber, the spirit of capitalism he describes, is "understandable . . . purely as a result of adaptation. . . . Whoever does not adapt his manner of life to the conditions of capitalistic success must go under, or at least cannot rise. But these are phenomena of a time in which modern capitalism has become dominant and has become emancipated from its old [religious] supports."[27]

Simple threat, force, and coercion do not, however, produce the sort of efficiency, the sort of productivity, that capitalism, especially in its finance-dominated form, demands. Grudging toleration of work, because it is inevitable, because one has no choice, does not an efficient worker make. Nor does fear of starvation while employed do much to enhance worker productivity. As Weber himself remarks, the early capitalist technique of lowering wages to get employees to work more just to support themselves did not have the intended effect: it simply enervated workers and prevented their intensive employment.[28] In general, one cannot get people to work that hard simply out of fear of what will happen to them if they don't, although a finance-dominated economic regime no doubt uses the precarious character of employment—constant fear of being downsized, becoming unemployed or underemployed—to its advantage. Instead of—or at least in addition to—fear employees have to be made to desire what their employment demands of them. Ideally, their desires should perfectly converge with that of the enterprise employing them. And here is where an ethic or spirit comes in. The question at root is one of subject formation—self-propelled, self-involved action—in line with capitalist demands. What your employer wants—the maximally efficient use of your capacities—is also what you want, what you yourself value, because you see it as part of your own individual efforts at self-realization, not something you are forced into by a foreign power through external imposition.

The Protestant ethic was the spirit of industrial capitalism in its Fordist varieties, where investments sunk in expensive equipment dedicated to the production of one thing meant mass production and mass consumption. That Protestant ethic was composed of a set of values in which hard work was a moral virtue, rewarded with good pay, where the expectation was for a kind of linear, gradual advancement along a single career track often at a single company—all of which suggested the reasonableness of delayed gratification and long-term commitment. The slow and steady pursuit of profit by firms—firms heavily invested in equipment capable of making only one thing and which therefore required huge sales of that one thing over the life of that equipment to be profitable—was matched by the slow and steady character of pursuit of success by employees dedicated to one life task.

This is in many respects no longer the spirit of contemporary, finance-dominated capitalism, which rewards flexibility and adaptability to constantly changing demands, where one might be expected to change jobs and tasks frequently and need to retool, where companies have no long-term commitment to you nor you to them. But in many other respects the new spirit of capitalism amounts to the continuation of a work ethic, in a heightened, intensified form. First of all, the link between effort and reward is not broken and assumes a highly moralized character. If one is not doing well, it is one's own fault—nobody else's. You just were not smart enough, for example, to read and understand the fine print on your mortgage documents. Second, one bears a completely individualized responsibility for both the costs and the rewards of one's behavior. No one is going to help you if you made a mistake in the sort of employment you chose to pursue or failed to accurately judge the risks of the actions you took in a futile effort to get ahead. Third, this individualized responsibility sets off a highly competitive relationship between oneself and others: your standing is determined over against others in a constantly expanding war of position. Pay, for instance, is geared to individual performance (and not to job description or seniority, which can be shared with others), and what counts as good performance continues to ratchet up, to escalate as your once superior performance is matched by that of others. Fourth, this ethic is intensified by being totalized. There is no "you" apart from it; it covers the entirety of life, at work and outside of it, and the whole of one's aspirations, in the way, for instance, that being indebted colonizes one's past, present, and future. Fifth and finally, the continuity of past, present, and future along a single linear employment trajectory in a traditional Protestant ethic also finds an insidious analogue in the new spirit of capitalism. A kind of unbreakable continuity exists between past, present, and future—they in fact collapse into one another, fuse with one another—in ways that make any radical break with the present order seem impossible. This is a constantly changing economic order or regime, requiring constant change from the participants in it, but one offering no escape from it; the future simply promises more of the same.

Précis of Chapters to Come

This time fusion, with its imagination-constricting effect, occurs in a variety of ways, which help organize the chapters to come. First, the discipline of debt makes present and future simple artifacts of a past promise; present and future collapse into a past that continues to make its demands and cannot be forgiven. Second, the constant demand for rapid, near immediate response to new developments makes past and future disappear. There is nothing but the present; the present monopolizes attention in ways that chain one to it, making one the prisoner of it. There is nothing but the present emergency for finance-disciplined employees; they are disciplined in much the same way poor people are. Without sufficient funds to get by, lacking any financial cushion, every challenge—even, say, a flat tire—threatens to become a crisis requiring all of one's immediate attention. Like the short-term preoccupations of corporations adapting to the time pressures posed by stock markets, one cannot plan for the future. The likely demands of the future recede from consciousness and in that sense collapse into the now, under the weight of the present emergency that requires immediate response and grabs one's full attention.

At the same time as there is nothing *but* the present, there is nothing *to* the present, to form the basis for decision-making with any temporal horizon. The present shrinks with the rapid turnover of changing circumstances to be addressed; things change at a moment's notice. Indeed, the economically significant present shrinks to something too short to be experienced. A billion dollars can be made in a nanosecond via computerized trading that arbitrages the difference in the values of similar financial instruments across different markets for them. As the scholar David Harvey observes, "Speed and the rapid reductions in the friction of distance and of turnover times . . . preclude time to imagine or construct alternatives other than those forced unthinkingly upon us as we rush to perform."[29]

Past, present, and future also tend to collapse into one another in secondary financial markets oriented to future value. On the one hand, present value is completely determined by expectations of future value; present value just *is* the discounted future. On the other hand, what future value will be is determined by and collapses into present expectation. As mentioned before, present expectation becomes a self-fulfilling prophecy on secondary markets: if everyone expects a stock's value to rise and buys it, its price on the stock market *will* rise.

The bottom line of all these temporal effects? No future can be imagined that would be radically different from the present. The result is a kind of totalization of capitalism itself; no future exists *outside* present capitalist arrangements.

What I, as a Christian theologian, attempt to do here is provide a Protestant anti-work ethic, by coming up with what I believe are good religious reasons for (1) breaking the link between a right to well-being and work; (2) breaking one's identification with one's "productive" self; and (3) breaking the time continuity, the time collapse, that constrains imaginative possibility under the current configuration of capitalism. What is perhaps now, unlike at the time when Weber was writing, an enclave in Fredric Jameson's sense, a self-contained cultural backwater of little obvious importance for how money is made nowadays, has, for that very reason, the capacity to be brought to bear against capitalism from outside it, in appropriate riposte to a system that purports to encompass the whole.[30] Although the current configuration of capitalism might not allow much room for imagining fundamental reforms from within it, one might yet radically break from it, in ways that make curiously apropos the inability of traditional utopias to account for agency or for the transition out of present circumstances in any coherent "historical or practical-political" manner. An "answer to . . . the conviction that no alternative is possible" comes "by forcing us to think the break itself, and not by offering a more traditional picture of what things would be like after the break."[31]

In keeping with such attempts at revolutionary alteration rather than simple internal reform, Christianity, I hope to show, is a religion of radical time discontinuity, promoting thereby expectations of radically disruptive transformation. For example, in contrast to a capitalism that requires via indebtedness an unbreakable continuity with one's past self, Christianity holds out hope of not being oneself any longer, as that is established by past and present. Such is the meaning of conversion to new life, of baptism as a death to the "old man" of sin. One remains the sinner one once was but the effects of sin are to be felt no longer. One can live life on a new basis, with freedom from the past. One breaks from oneself by way of some dramatic upheaval, a drastic change from one mode of being to another, a radical transition that tears the self away from the self as it has been to new life, to rebirth, dramatized as a figurative passage through death. As Foucault says, following Pierre Hadot, in contrasting Christian conversion with conversion as understood in the Hellenistic and Roman culture of Christianity's birth, "A fundamental element of Christian conversion is renunciation of oneself, dying to oneself, and being reborn in a different self and a new form which, as it were, no longer has anything to do with the earlier self in its being, its mode of being, in its habits or its ethos."[32]

Even apart from sin, Christian hopes tend to be quite extravagant. To be saved is to have a radically transfigured self, beyond anything possible for one as a mere finite creature. To be saved is to be elevated beyond oneself, so as to participate in the very life of God, to share in the very properties of God's own life—eternal life. It is to leave behind simply finite life, one's entire life as one has known it up until this point. It is, in short, to be deified, to be made other than oneself in the most radical way possible, as that reflects the utter difference, the infinite gulf, between human and divine.

To be saved therefore does not mean, as it so often did in Hellenistic and Roman culture, to be preserved from harm, to be guarded, protected, shielded, from a threatening danger, so as to remain in one's existing condition; it does not mean to be kept safe so as to remain in the condition one was in previously.[33] It means instead to lead a fundamentally disrupted life—if not (wholly) now then in hopes of a future that will be nothing like one's experience of past and present.

Movement across a disjunction of this radical sort—between who we are in the past and present, on the one hand, and who we will be, on the other—requires divine agency. *God* moves us from here to there. To break with oneself requires more than oneself. It has to be done *for* one. What one gets to—where one gets to—is therefore not a matter of one's own performance but more likely (especially given sin) a reversal of what one would achieve by one's own power. It therefore becomes very hard to say, as the new spirit of capitalism would counsel, that one's future good fortune has been merited, that one is individually responsible for it.

Besides its account of conversion, salvation, and the place of divine agency in securing them, Christian understandings of God are also potentially disruptive of the time collapse typical of the new spirit of capitalism. Christian understandings of God, as those developed in the early church under the pressure of extravagant claims made about Christ, do not make God a God of this world by closely associating divinity with any particular feature of it, such as its order, the reason at work in things. God is beyond the world, nothing like any part of it; God is not an instance of any sort of thing to be found in the world. Conformity to God therefore does not lead to conformity to the way things are. It does not mean, for example (as it did for ancient Stoicism), aligning one's individual aims with, submerging them into, harmonizing them with a universal given order of things, in much the way the new spirit of capitalism counsels a perfect convergence between one's own desires and that of the broader firm or the market generally, as that establishes the cosmological givens of present-day global capitalism.

What might it mean for this in some ways very old spirit of Christianity to confront the new spirit of capitalism? Much more is said about this in the chapters to come.

2

Chained to the Past

One major way finance-dominated capitalism organizes time so as to structure human subjectivity and hinder the critique of capitalism is by magnifying the significance of the past for present and future conduct. What present and future can hold is rigidly and comprehensively determined by a past decision—whether one's own or someone else's—concerning what is to come. The past meets one as a personally obligating command or order proscribing present and future conduct in an unrelenting way that permits of no breaks or ruptures. Present and future are captive to the past.

The manner in which profits are generated through debt in finance-dominated capitalism is one way this kind of temporal effect on human subjectivity is brought about. Debt is increasingly used by cash-strapped individuals to make up for what finance-dominated corporations and governments no longer provide: a living wage, on the one hand, and guarantees of education and more than simple survival in times of trouble, on the other. One's paycheck routinely runs out before the end of the month, requiring one to amass credit card debt or take out payday loans, at exorbitant rates, to make ends meet. The government no longer provides money for an education but facilitates taking out the necessary loans to pay for it. Indeed, forced into austerity measures by their creditors, states increasingly refuse responsibility for government spending to alleviate recessions; responsibility for kick-starting economic growth shifts to individuals who can spend beyond their now meager means in hard times only by taking on personal debt.[1] The effects of this sort of forced debt—to meet basic needs under conditions of hardship—are constrictive rather than expansive of future possibility, extractive of already existing value rather than productive of new value. This sort of debt simply chains individuals in highly restrictive ways to the past in which they assumed it. And all this, as I suggest in this chapter, is not inadvertent but a deliberate mechanism of profit generation through debt under finance-dominated capitalism.

Much the same temporal effects on human subjectivity come about by way of workplace restructuring to meet stock-market demands for maximum profitability at the lowest possible cost, that is, management practices that accord with concerns for shareholder value. The inexorability of past decisions becomes the way to get the most out of the few workers retained on payroll and the way to force other companies working at your behest to squeeze their workers.

By agreeing to take out a loan or perform a task for one's employer, one promises to abide by, and therefore assumes personal responsibility for fulfilling, an expectation regarding future conduct that increasingly takes on the character of an inexorable demand. Short of simple exit (by declaring bankruptcy or quitting one's job), continuing on the way set by a prior decision to which one has committed oneself, for example by accepting employment, means working for a future in strict conformity with a past decision regarding it. Every present is past preoccupied, and nothing more is to be expected in the future than what the past has already laid down in the form of anticipation. One is bound in the present, so to speak, by a memory of the promised future, by a future target set in the past (whether that target takes the form of eventual loan repayment or a work performance benchmark) to be honored in one's conduct at every moment, come what may, whatever else the future might bring.[2]

How the Past Becomes an Inexorable Demand

Past decisions have an inexorable quality here in part because, once signed onto, they are unalterable and inflexible, subject to no fundamental renegotiation of their terms due to unforeseen contingencies in the lives of borrower or workers. Indeed, making the decision to sign onto the initial terms—say, agreeing to pay off a car loan in ten years—often simply means assuming responsibility oneself for managing all future contingencies in line with that final objective. Failing to manage one's life, with all its risks and perils, in ways that allow one to pay off one's debts therefore means paying the price oneself: one's car is repossessed, with nothing to show for all those prior payments, perhaps far in excess—because of high interest rates—of the car's actual value.

Fixing the objective without assuming responsibility for the means is typically part of the take it or leave it quality of the demanding past in finance-dominated capitalism: do whatever it takes to meet the specified target; how one gets there is one's own business so long as the target itself, which remains essentially intact and unaltered, is met within the time allowed.[3] The work team charged with designing a new product line in two weeks is thus free to manage itself, as is the subcontractor required by a lead company to deliver X number of goods of the specified quality at time T. The responsibility for such matters is simply handed over by the company to others. Because the workers or subcontractors are self-managing in responding to company demands, whatever eventualities impede satisfactory completion of company orders are laid at their feet, with highly moralizing effects. Expectations of future performance in this way become unsparing and unforgiving: failures to meet previously set targets, whatever their provenance, whether the problems were foreseeable or not, whether under worker control or not, are treated as equally punishable offenses, meriting outright dismissal or loss of any future contract for work.

The past also becomes an inexorable demand under finance-dominated capitalism in that past targets for future performance often seem nearly impossible to meet and therefore have a highly constrictive effect on possibilities for present and future conduct: everything else needs to be sacrificed to meet them.[4]

Demands that the past makes on the future tend to become difficult to meet in part because of a mismatch between this way of structuring time and others equally typical of finance-dominated capitalism. Even as present and future conduct is bound by past decision, one finds oneself in an extremely volatile environment that makes anticipation of the future highly unreliable. One commits oneself to continuous mortgage payments, month after month, for the next thirty years at the same time as work becomes increasingly precarious, as the likelihood of being laid off at some point in one's working life or holding merely contingent, part-time, or on-call employment at irregular weekly or monthly wages for most of one's life increases.

One's steady livelihood is far from assured even as demands from the past in the form of debt seem to presuppose it.[5]

Similarly, workers are chained to the past even as their employers are freed from it, retaining the right to revoke at will the initial decision to hire them (as is the case in the United States), altering time schedules and shifting the targets that put demands on workers' time to reflect unanticipated changes in market conditions. What makes meeting a target difficult—having to manage constantly changing conditions over the course of time necessary to bring a product or service to market—becomes the responsibility of the workforce. At least temporarily inflexible targets are required to bring any product or service to market; the costs of managing the constantly changing conditions under which those targets are pursued become the responsibility of others, a self-managing workforce or subcontractor.

The difficulties faced by workers in managing volatility here are not simply the flip side of their being successfully avoided by others: once a target, formulated and reformulated to reflect rapidly changing conditions, is finally set and can no longer be changed, somebody needs to cope with the impediments posed to meeting it by unforeseen eventualities. How about you rather than me? The past-refusing culture of liquidity, otherwise typical of finance-dominated capitalism, has itself the direct effect of chaining workers more thoroughly to the past in production processes.

Finance-dominated capitalism is a culture of liquidity in that most profit-generating mechanisms within it are predicated upon the refusal of constraint from past decisions. Institutional mechanisms are put in place that allow all past commitments to be revisited and revised.[6] So, for example, stock exchanges allow stock prices to be constantly reevaluated and participants in those stock markets to sell previously purchased stock at any time in response to these changing price signals. By way of secondary markets such as stock exchanges, any past decision to commit funds can be cashed out whenever one likes, in the search for more profitable investment opportunities. Mortgages made to homeowners can be repackaged as bonds and sold to investors, the money originally loaned to those homeowners immediately returning thereby to the banks for reuse. Assumption of risk by past decisions to loan are now no longer borne by the originators of those loans but transferred to bondholders, who can similarly pass responsibility for, say, any default risk they incur to those willing to insure such bonds.

Corporations disciplined by stockholder demands for maximum profitability also typically try to achieve greater profitability by breaking constraints on production posed by sunk costs. Using so-called post-Fordist techniques of lean and just-in-time production to maximize profit, corporations avoid all immobile capital expenditures that would tie their hands regarding future production, whether that immobile capital takes the form of stockpiles of components or warehouses full of finished products awaiting consumer orders or machines that can make only one thing. What they have already produced or already purchased by way of equipment no longer limits the capacity of companies to respond to changes in consumer demand. They have produced only as much as is necessary to meet current orders and are therefore not faced with the dismal prospect of trying to sell more of what people no longer seem to want to buy. And the machines they have can be retooled to produce new product lines, so as to capture untapped markets or respond to changes in consumer sentiment. Nothing sits around and goes to waste, remaining unused or unsold for any length of time, and the same machines can constantly churn out products of one sort or another, switching product lines as necessary.

These same post-Fordist techniques for maximum utilization of investment typically enforce human capital mobility—what they ask of machines they also ask of people. For example, rather than being constrained in what they can produce in the future by past decisions to hire people with a single specialty or competence, companies require workers to be able to perform a multitude of tasks, tasks that can be varied at will depending on changing production requirements. Thus, workers need to know not simply how to work with a specific machine but how to perform preventative maintenance on it, how to change its components to alter its productive capacities, and how to use it just as efficiently for those newly enabled purposes. The multitasking of machines is matched by the multitasking of workers.

While all these post-Fordist techniques prevent a company's productive capacities from being hemmed in by past investment decisions, they have the opposite effect on workers due to the extremely tight flow in the production process they bring about.[7] Preceding parts of the production process take on a more demanding character under post-Fordist conditions; what others have done before now requires more of the worker and in that sense becomes more difficult to address, compelling greater effort. Compared with earlier assembly line production, more intensive exertion is now required from workers because the lack of stockpiles removes all slack from the production process, thereby eliminating (in principle) all idle or down time. One no longer waits to add value to what others have been too slow in producing nor relaxes by virtue of having produced much more than is needed by workers further down the production chain. By way of computerized technologies that match orders to production in real time and regulate parts of the production process accordingly, bottlenecks, formed by the under- or overproduction of components and final products, no longer occur to interrupt production flow, either in-house or on the way to customers. Finished products, for example, come into the warehouse as soon as they are to go out, requiring a constant flow of work from those who transport stock. Workers are in constant movement because the product is. And when they are at work they are always working; the same computerized technologies that match production to customer orders in real time mean workers can be called in only when needed. Even breakdowns through mechanical malfunctions occur less frequently to interrupt the otherwise continuous flow. The routine maintenance that workers do at their own workstations whenever customer orders flag is designed to prevent such interruptions. And when breakdowns do happen the workers who run the machines can immediately provide the fix themselves rather than waiting around for help to arrive. Moreover, in contrast to earlier forms of production line assembly where slacking off could be hidden, any lapse in the constant exertion required by tight flow is immediately evident to all; because the flow has no slack in it, flow is fragile and unforgiving of failures in compliance. One misstep and the whole line stops. In all these ways, the past—starting with the initial customer order and proceeding through all the production stages prior to the one for which the worker is responsible— takes on the character of a continuously exercised, inescapable, and unrelenting pressure.

Put more simply and more generally to cover all sorts of work and not simply assembly line production and distribution flows, in finance-dominated capitalism the setting of nearly impossible demands is an intentional strategy for extracting

the greatest possible effort from workers. Pressure from shareholders for maximum profitability means making do with less;
payrolls are cut to the bone to reduce costs as much as possible,
and that means fewer workers are now required to perform the
work that a far greater number did before. Almost any future
target—say, any of the ones typical of company production
prior to such cost-cutting measures—becomes more difficult
to achieve under such conditions, requiring maximum effort
from the few employees who remain. But again under market
pressures for increasing returns on investment, companies also
typically set ever more difficult tasks for their employees in the
effort to enforce greater productivity in performance, their more
efficient use of time, their doing more at a quicker pace. The
tasks workers have been asked to perform become, for example,
much more complex and detail oriented, and the timeframes
for their completion tighter. What one has been asked to do
becomes, in short, nearly impossible to achieve unless one is
willing to work constantly and with enormous intensity. Workers are made more productive the more one now asks of them.

Setting nearly impossible demands is also a typical
mechanism for cost cutting in companies that meet stockholder pressures for maximum profitability by reorganizing
their operations according to a core-periphery model.[8] The
most profitable parts—the core parts—of the business are retained in-house while the least profitable ones are outsourced
or made the responsibility of subcontractors, so as to form a
periphery around the lead company purchasing services or
production inputs. Design and marketing teams and the front
office pulling in the deals are the ones adding the most value
and are responsible most directly for making all the money;
they are to be retained as company employees. The janitors and
maintenance staff, along with those performing data entry and

providing payroll services—all workers performing inessential functions—are mere costs of production or final service provision, to be outsourced or employed by other companies even if they work in-house. All the parts that compose the final product, that is, all the inputs that form costs of production, all supporting functions that amount to costs of final service provision—such as legal research and market analysis—can be subcontracted or outsourced. Indeed, every aspect of production between design and sale—the actual assembly of parts, every function that enables front-office deal-making—is to be subcontracted or outsourced.

All these subsidiary products and services that contribute to the lead company's own eventual provision of a product or service—whether it be an Apple computer or a bond issue—still have to be paid for, but their costs have now been minimized: they cost far less than they would have if the work had been done by the company's own employees. This is simply a function of market competition: all the many companies capable of providing what the lead company requires compete with one another for its business, thereby driving down prices. If janitors were paid in-house, their pay would for a variety of reasons be far higher than if they were supplied by other companies on the open market. Given the number of those companies (there are very few entrance hurdles to cleaning service startups), the lead company can easily bargain down the price for those services. Indeed, pressured by shareholders for maximum profitability, lead companies can—more or less easily depending on their market share and the number of competing sub-firms capable of providing quality product—set a take-it-or-leave-it rock bottom price beyond which they refuse to budge.

The profit margins on these sub-firms are typically quite low in any case. That is in great part why direct responsibility for providing products and services has been shed by the lead company. But now those profit margins are forced even lower by lead company price demands, to a near breaking-point level if at all possible, beyond which lies simple failure to return any profit at all. Besides forcing lower the wages of employees of subcontractors—employees are often paid below minimum wage—the near-impossible price demands made by lead companies put pressure on subcontractors to hire the minimum number of workers and to work them as hard as possible, often in violation of labor laws. For example, employees may routinely be forced to work before and after their official shifts without pay.

Pressured to reduce payroll costs, subcontractors may also employ the same core-periphery cost-cutting strategies of lead companies. They may become, for example, merely the brand organizers for collections of smaller cleaning outfits, and in that way increase their own profit margins by squeezing those of their franchisees. Profits are in this way forced ever lower as one proceeds down the resulting nested chain of suppliers: the closer to the lead company, the greater the profit margins, with the lead company itself making an outsized return on investment. And as the profit margins shrink along the chain, the greater is the pressure put on workers to make do with less and to work ever harder. While the lead company itself and its direct suppliers make sufficient profits to hire more employees and work them less intensely, it is simply part of this business model not to do so. The target of maximum profitability set by Wall Street forbids it. In this way nearly impossible demands for maximum exertion from workers come to mark the whole supply chain from top to bottom.

The setting of nearly impossible demands for profit-generating purposes is also typical of the way debt functions in finance-dominated capitalism. One might think loans would be profitable only when they have a good chance of being paid off. Loans are theoretically made in order to be repaid, with profits generated by way of the difference between the interest payments due to the creditor over time and the costs of generating the funds loaned. If profits are primarily predicated on repayment, one would not want to stretch the borrower's sources of income so far through indebtedness as to jeopardize that repayment, and one would loan with the expectation that borrowed funds would prove profitable to the borrower, since those profits might prove the prime source of funds for loan repayment. In conditions of finance-dominated capitalism, to the contrary, difficulty in meeting the demands to pay the loans off seems a major part of their point: indeed, maximum difficulty, pushing to the edge of borrower insolvency, becomes something of an ideal.

This is in part because profit is generated not by the slow trickle of interest and principal payments by borrowers to loan originators but by repackaging loans into bonds for immediate sale to investors. The higher the interest rate paid to investors in such bonds, the greater their attractiveness, and this requires the interest rates on the original loans to be as high as possible, near but not tipping over into what is beyond a borrower's ability to pay. Financially strapped borrowers with low credit scores become prime lending targets; they can be charged higher interest rates (along with hefty fees) to compensate for greater default risk.[9]

Their actual defaulting would not be a good thing, at least if it happened quickly across the board so as to spook investors. To delay the inevitable, more money can be lent to persons at risk of defaulting—for instance, beyond the value of any collateral at the time of the initial loan so that the extra is itself available to pay the interest on the loan until it runs out. And when those extra funds do evaporate, the initial loan can be rolled over, thereby adding to one's original indebtedness. The secondhand car one bought with borrowed money at high interest rates breaks down. One cannot get to work without it, and absent a paycheck one is in jeopardy of defaulting on the payments still owed on it. So one takes out an even bigger loan at even higher interest rates to pay off the first loan and purchase another car, and so on.[10] One is unable to make ends meet at the end of the month on one's meager salary as the employee of a cleaning company franchise, and therefore one takes out a payday loan at sky-high interest rates. But if one struggled to make ends meet without a loan, doing so now becomes even more difficult with loan payments to make on top of regular expenses for food and housing, requiring a new loan of a larger amount at perhaps even higher rates. And so it goes. Indefinite extension of indebtedness until eventual default—at some point the diversion of funds that might otherwise be used for food and shelter from people of limited means reaches its limit in default. Indefinite extension with that ultimate end— being chained to one's debt until defeated by it—seems endemic to the primary mechanism of profit generation here.

Rather than expanding possibilities for profit on the part of borrowers as one primary avenue for generating revenues to pay back loans, debt here as elsewhere in finance-dominated capitalism has a contractive and expropriating effect. Debt means poor people find it harder rather than easier to live well. Clearly payday loans, and loans for consumption purposes generally when assumed by cash-strapped borrowers, do not lend a hand out of poverty but help keep people in it.[11] Money that could have been used to pay for food and housing now goes to service a debt whose high interest rate prevents one from ever hoping to repay. Just that much less—in the amount equal to what is demanded for debt servicing—remains available for essential expenses, forcing extremes of self-management from the poor in the effort to cope with increasing extremes of austerity demanded by growing debt. It is all the same to one's creditors whether the loan for that used car actually expanded one's opportunities by helping one get a better job in places underserved by public transport. It is just as well that one did not get the job and the car was repossessed by the dealership to be recirculated to other borrowers on the same basis, with the same dismal outcomes—for them. Rather than leading to a better job, that increasing debt made one willing to accept any job, no matter how poorly paid and backbreaking the working conditions.[12]

The assumption of debt by government has the same contractive and constricting effects, making the past a dead weight rather than an opening to a future beyond it.[13] Revenues from taxation are designed to enable government service provision—in the form of parks and infrastructure construction, educational opportunities, and programs to ensure the well-being of its citizens. Generating revenue through debt on the open market has the opposite effect, especially when such debt is issued to cover shortfalls in tax revenue. Less money is available for service provision, and more money is diverted to debt servicing; government service provision has to contract by an amount equal to that required for debt servicing rather than being helped to expand by way of it. This contraction of service provision is not merely, moreover, a necessary evil in times of economic contraction that bring a slowdown in tax revenues, a necessary but unfortunate effect of stagnant growth. It is viewed by the community of creditors as a salutary development in any case, whatever the economic conditions, insofar as it forces government efficiencies via cost cutting—fewer government employees and redundant agencies, indeed less service provision altogether (which in the case of government is a cost against revenue rather than, as in the service industry, a source of profit). Pressured by the debt they have assumed in hard times, governments are to be run more productively, which reassures their creditors about their likely solvency in the future and continued ability to make payments on their bonds. Only efficiently run governments, which means governments run like finance-dominated corporations so as to cut costs to the bone, are deemed credit-worthy on the open market.

Indeed, the model here is the way companies are forced into efficiencies by difficulty servicing debt.[14] When companies are taken over by investors trying to make money through their purchase and sale, those companies are saddled with the debt used to purchase them. And that puts immediate pressure on their revenue streams. Prior to being taken over by, say, a private equity firm that borrowed money to purchase it using the company itself as collateral, the company may have sold enough to pay costs of production, meet employee payrolls, and turn a profit. Now, because it also has to service the debt used to acquire it, its revenues are quite possibly no longer sufficient for such purposes. The company can try to increase revenues dramatically but that is difficult to do and takes time; the quick fix is to cut costs, most easily by way of reducing company employees and lowering the pay and benefits of the ones retained. In this way employees are expropriated in order to pay company creditors. When the company is eventually brought onto the market, sold by way of newly issued stock as a publicly traded company, these greater efficiencies through cost cutting, which assumption of debt has helped force through, are taken by investors as a good sign; the market valuation of the company is more than it was before, and the private equity firm cashes out, relinquishing its ownership at a profit. Again, this happens at the expense of downsized workers and the workers who remain, now forced to work harder simply to stay in place.

Finally, the demands of the past are inexorable here—whether by way of debt or workplace organization—in that the whole of life is consumed in the attempt to meet them.[15] The whole of life must be dedicated to their service just because they are so difficult to meet otherwise. Debt when it is forced by need and not simply a matter of convenience—I could pay by cash or check for everything I purchase but choose, for simplicity's sake, to rack up a single credit card bill whose balance I pay off every month—always has this disciplining effect on all of life, inclusive of both work and leisure. Can I afford to quit my job given my debts? Or to complain about working conditions if that would threaten my yearly bonus? Should I really have this expensive cup of coffee or buy this brand-name sweater for my child given the growing monthly minimum payment on my credit card? Unlike other contractual obligations in commercial exchange or in productive activities that involve the sale of labor time, no aspect of life is immune to debt's pressures. Relations with one's creditors are not broken off at the moment of contract settlement as they are in relations of exchange, nor do one's obligations in assuming debt end when one clocks out of the factory. One has promised instead to organize the whole of one's life as both a worker and consumer to meet the demands of debt; every aspect of life is potentially relevant to one's ability to service it. And will in fact become so relevant the more difficult it is to make the payments on that debt.

But work demands tend to become just as life consuming as debt under finance-dominated forms of company reorganization. Because demands set in the past for future performance are so difficult to meet and because there is no down time at work that could be used to catch up on work that one has fallen behind on, work tends to bleed into time off.[16] One spends longer hours at work trying to complete tasks on time; it's after hours, one should be at home but one stays at work instead until the wee hours of the morning in an attempt to meet a deadline. And time away from the office, on nights and weekends, is increasingly dedicated to completing what simply couldn't be finished there, try as one might. The extreme pressures of past demands on future performance in this way come to colonize every waking moment.

Christian Views of the Past

Given the generally unfortunate character of this temporal structuring of human subjectivity within finance-dominated capitalism, one might, with Michel Foucault, try to disrupt it by scanning the historical record for different models of human subjectivity and thereby contest the inevitability of this particular way of structuring relations to the past. Such alternative models of human subjectivity could put this one in its place as a contingent development, but they might also, if viable now— if supported by forms of community life extending into the present—offer potential avenues of active resistance.[17]

I believe that certain Christian ways of structuring the temporal dimensions of human subjectivity stand out in this regard. They do not just differ from it (as many other models presumably do to some degree) but pose the starkest possible contrast with the temporal structuring just outlined. Rather than determining a future target, the past is problematized and often radically so: one is counseled to repudiate it. One is not to be who one was before, the sort of person one committed oneself to being or becoming in the past. Moreover, in contrast to expectations of some seamless way from here to there, from past target to future realization, for a variety of religious reasons sharp discontinuities are properly thought to break the hold of the past on present and future conduct. This may be partly a function of the disreputable character of the past: past and future conduct cannot be joined in any continuous fashion just to the degree the past is what is to be left behind. But even when past targets remain in some sense normative for future conduct, something about that target prevents expectation of continuous progress toward it, often requiring something of a discontinuous leap across a divide.

The past of course is sometimes considered by Christians to be something of great value, indeed taken to represent an ideal to which present and future conduct are to conform. One is to identify oneself with a human past that was originally perfect in Paradise, an Eden in which human life perfectly matched divine intentions for it. Or, one existed oneself (along with all other individuals) in an ideal state in the mind of God prior to being created in the world as we know it, a world of change and bodies. The past becomes a norm exerting pressure on future conduct just to the extent it has been lost. Where one has been but is no longer determines where one is going. Being saved means returning to lost origins, recovering the ideal form of oneself as God originally knew it, or the state of Adam's conformity with God before the fall. Who one was, whether in God or proleptically in Adam, is who one is to become again with God's help. One is to exert oneself to the utmost now, by way of God's grace, to bring one's life in its entirety back into line with that.

Much of this is simply a Platonic legacy, following in Christian form the past preoccupations of a Platonic model for structuring human subjectivity. There exists an ideal for human life to be imitated now that was once enjoyed to the full and that one can return to one day. One lived the life of the gods before falling to earth, either literally or figuratively, and the struggle now is to return to the life one once knew.

Such a model does bring with it a certain suspicion of the past and a disjunctive temporality that breaks continuity with the future (even though that future has the form of the past). Everything since the time of original perfection is devalued, and in that sense almost all of the past, beyond the past at its origin, is in some significant sense to be discarded, left behind. All that one has been since that time of origin, all the commitments to worldly matters that have made one what one is since the fall, are ultimately to be repudiated. There might exist a continuous ladder back to the past, made possible by the way ideal forms are variously manifest in the material world—one moves by stages, for Plato himself, from beautiful boys to beautiful ideas—but at some point one jumps suddenly out of this whole realm of embodied preoccupations into a different one, an intelligible world where one contemplates pure forms themselves. Depending on the state into which one has fallen and the seriousness of the impediments it presents for return, no perfectly continuous process of return might be possible, requiring divine intervention to bring future into line with the past. Simple ignorance of origins, for example, might prevent return apart from a saving knowledge brought to the material world from without, as in Gnosticism. Or, the state of the light within material existence might be so fragmented, so dissipated, as to obstruct all efforts to collect itself without a new infusion of light from beyond, as in some Christian forms of Manichaeism. Apart from grace one is not even an agent of the light struggling against the evil of material embodiment; one becomes that only with grace, in a kind of switch from nothing to something.

But the close association of ideal self with divinity within a Platonic model tends to mean that what one was is never fully lost and that therefore the way back to origins is in principle and most fundamentally a matter of continuous progress. One did not simply exist in a divine state originally; one has a divine nature. One is not simply a once-upon-a-time visitor but a proper member of the divine realm, being oneself in some measure pure spirit, pure light, pure form. Because divinity constitutes one's essential identity, it cannot be fully lost in one's fallen state. For all the corruption of character that may have prompted the fall or that may ensue once fallen, one remains fundamentally what one was before, one's divine self, but now in a very bad situation or hostile circumstances. When one repudiates what one has become, one therefore is not repudiating oneself, certainly not in any wholesale way, but rather the conditions under which one presently exists in their unwholesome effects.

Remaining divine in some significant sense, one retains, moreover, the means for return to a state in which one's divinity will be fully manifest and free from taint. What one is to become, in other words, builds on what one remains. Salvation often indeed suggests nothing more than a change of state without need for any fundamental change in character—the process of salvation taken to involve simple purification from foreign influences, the stripping away of external accretions, that enables one to become more fully what one already essentially is—to effect a kind of consolidation of who one has always truly been. Bringing one's present and future into strict alignment with one's past self, salvation means one's past self is now protected from harm, delivered from threat.

The Christian affirmation that humans have a merely created, nondivine nature means to the contrary of all this that if humans enjoyed some sort of perfect unity with God's intentions for them before their creation or at their first creation in Paradise, what they enjoyed then can be completely lost. The perfection that was once theirs was not theirs by nature but accrued to them by virtue of that very unity with God; it was a perfection not of human nature but of the state human nature was in. If sin breaks that relationship with God and radically changes the conditions of human existence, perfection can simply be replaced by total corruption. Made to exist in unity with God, humans without God have their lives turned upside down; they become the opposite of what they should be. If they were once light in and through God's light, they now find themselves in utter darkness.

Salvation then means the complete repudiation of what one has become through sin. What has organized one's whole life in its turning away from God is now to be forfeited. One must simply renounce what one has become by turning away from that past of sin and becoming something entirely new: humans, once lost in their complete corruption without God, now found with God (because of what Christ accomplishes) to their unsurpassable benefit. Rather than being some continuous process, the passage from one state to another is like a passage through death; one dies to one's old self (an old self whose life amounted to a kind of death) in order to be born again into another life. Such a rebirth means no resuscitation of the corpse but entrance into an entirely new manner of human existence, enlivened by God's own life. Such a passage is therefore enabled by nothing that remains the creature's own under conditions of sin, living as it does a kind of death without God, but comes by way of grace alone, the grace of Christ who reconciles, who brings back into unity with God what has been separated from God to its absolute detriment.

The conversion, or turning away and to, at issue here is a kind of participation in Christ's own death and resurrection, a dying to the world and rising with him, and in its extremity is akin to one's own death and resurrection to come. One's life of sin can no more contribute to one's new life to come than can one's body rotting away in the grave to one's resurrection. The life force completely lost by way of one's own death, the utter corruption of the grave, will be made up for by the empowering Spirit of God's own life to come.

Or the passage in question might be likened to the release or cancellation of an enslaving debt, one that is otherwise impossible to remit by way of one's own resources. Sin can itself be considered a sort of unpaid debt in that one has failed to make good on what God has provided, defaulted on the obligation to act in accord with God's good intentions, in ways that can no longer be remedied through one's own efforts, every such attempt simply bringing one into greater debt because of one's fundamental corruption. Sin in this way eventuates in a kind of debt-slavery, imprisoning one within the debt that is sin itself, making it impossible to repay, a form of unrelenting bondage. The transition out of debt is consequently quite abrupt; no gradual repayment from within prison walls brings about one's release from its prison. That release comes suddenly from unexpected quarters, in ways that cancel one's own need to pay. Christ becomes the strange currency or treasure that allows one now to make good on one's obligations to God, and in that way Christ breaks one's bondage to sin.[18]

The fact of such serious gaps in the passage from old life to new is made clear in peculiar forms of Christian self-narration: retrospective ones. What is to come cannot be told prospectively, that is, looking forward from the standpoint of the past and present toward the future to come. Because of the unexpected twists and turns to come, there is no way to get from here to there starting from the past and making it the basis for a projection about what the future will hold. Only from the standpoint of an otherwise unanticipated outcome can one look back and retell the story of one's life in ways that make sense of such an outcome, by interjecting where necessary elements of complete surprise. Now that one knows how one has ended up—saved from sin—one can see how, unbeknownst to one and often contrary to one's own intentions, God was working on one's behalf to bring one where one otherwise could not have brought oneself.

Augustine's *Confessions* would be the model here. It may be that a retrospective telling allows Augustine to smooth over his past history by reading into his past what he only realized later, so that his conversion to Christianity seems more the outcome of a continuous process of intellectual inquiry than it in fact was (at least if one takes at face value some of his other writings prior to the *Confessions*).[19] But such a narrative form, looking back at the past from the future that has now arrived, also allows that future to be an unanticipated one from the standpoint of the past: how could someone so sunk in sin as Augustine was ever have been expected to end up where he did, a bishop? The radical nature of the change seems very much like the creation from nothing outlined in the last books of the *Confessions*.

The interpretive process here—from future to past in order to make sense of the future's unexpected character—is similar to typological readings of God's workings over the whole of salvation history, as that spans both Old and New Testaments.[20] Events recounted in the Old Testament can be seen to refer to events in Christ's life but only after the latter events have happened and from their standpoint. Such a retrospective reading is necessary because the later events follow the pattern or form of the earlier ones in highly unexpected ways that simply could not be anticipated beforehand. No one could have predicted, for example, that a man identified with God would come to stand in the place of Temple practices, doing what they were originally designed to do and in that way repeating their form—removing impediments to Israel's conformity with God's laws—but in an entirely novel way, through the shedding of his own blood rather than animal sacrifice.

Such a narrative practice—reading backward from later to earlier—can obviously be used to smooth over the gaps between old and new, by reading the later into the earlier in ways that evacuate Israel's past of any independent significance. According to that way of looking at things, this is what the earlier narratives about ancient Israelite practice always meant or referred to; their Christian sense is their only significance, simply replacing, in supersessionist fashion, any sense they might have had before. The surprise of what is to come would thus be lost: what happened before now becomes something like a transparent prediction of future events; the future simply conforms to the past's true sense.

But the need for retrospective reading is often, to the contrary, predicated on a disjunction between earlier and later that allows earlier events to have their own distinctive significance. It is not simply that earlier stories take on a new, unexpected significance in light of what happened in Christ's life later on. The meaningfulness of those later events in Christ's life also depends on the distinctive sense of earlier events in their own time.[21] However surprising it might be, the New Testament identification of Jesus with bread from heaven, for example, makes little sense apart from a prior understanding of what manna meant within the story of Israel's escape from Egypt. That later identification with Christ gains much of its meaning from past events in virtue of their having already happened in the particular way they did. Those past events have their own significance within their own storied contexts and for that reason need not point, in and of themselves, to anything more to come. In the manner in which God's people were fed in the desert, *God* may have had Christ in mind, that surprising new twist to come in God's ongoing efforts to remain faithful to Israel, but that is no reason to assume those later events were somehow contained prospectively in it in ways that would have been evident to earlier authors of such stories or their audiences.[22] The same God working in similarly surprising ways— God works in highly surprising ways in the Old Testament too—establishes continuity between Jesus and the bread that fed the Israelites as they wandered in the desert, so that the significance of bread in that earlier story does not have the burden of establishing such continuity itself.

Because it is God who works in surprising ways to bridge the gap between earlier and later, the lack of any obvious internal continuity of meaning between the past and what is to come can be quite extreme without jeopardizing the intelligibility of the story told. Similarities of formal pattern may remain while the import of that recurrence radically shifts. Thus, Isaac's willingness to be slaughtered means the end of child sacrifice in Israel, while Christ's willingness to die brings Temple sacrifice itself to an end. There is continuity here but continuity that includes within it radical disjunction. Indeed, it is not unusual for Christians to claim that Christ recapitulates the patterns of prior history by reversing them: the story of Adam is retold in Christ but with perfect obedience taking the place of the former's utter sin.

Ways of making a coherent narrative out of radically disjunctive pasts and futures are also typical in Christian forms of self-narration. Split into two by conversion, Christian self-narration obviously cannot amount to a tale of an incrementally cumulative career in which what is to come builds in continuous, predictable fashion on what precedes it. Marked as it is by conversion, the coherence of Christian character cannot be narrated in terms of ongoing conformity to the same fundamental choice of oneself, from the start of one's life to its finish: one is X sort of person, and one's aim is to be more so, the best X one can be. If Christians have a character, it is from any normal point of view a character-destroying character, a character structured to expect and promote its own fundamental revision: the fundamental choices of oneself that organized one's life before are no longer to organize it.[23] It is a very odd sort of character, then, but a structured, organized character nonetheless. One's manner of relating to oneself may not take the form of a cumulative career in habitual conformity to a single, established character over the course of one's lifetime, but neither, in virtue of that fact, need one's manner of relating to oneself, past and present, break apart into simple incoherence: one was one sort of person before and now an entirely different sort of person, across some unbridgeable divide. For all the discontinuity—one's life was lost to God apart from Christ and now regained in him—one's past self remains indelible now in the form of one's having been it. Neither simply continuous nor simply discontinuous with who one is now, it will ever be one's denied identity.[24] It remains *one's own* past, oneself in the form of an ongoing disidentification with it, the past that one constantly struggles against.

Conversion is in this way never over; it is not a one-time event one leaves behind. It effects no simple break with a past now forgotten but means entering into an extended "state of break" whereby one constantly turns away from what remains a force in one's life. As Foucault notes, "*Metanoia* is a constant dimension of the life of the Christian. This movement by which one turns round must be maintained. It is not only a break but a state."[25] This conversion story, in which one's past continues to figure, becomes in other words the story of one's entire life. It narrates not simply an all-important moment in which one's life changed course but turns into one's whole life story, spanning every one of its moments.

Indeed, one is even now and, short of the eschaton, ever will be that sinner one was then, despite having been united again with God in Christ. What is radically different—the character of one's relationship with God in the past apart from Christ and now with him—permits one's remaining much as one was until that day when one will finally become holy as God is holy. United to Christ one has one's righteousness in Christ, in virtue simply of what he is, until Christ's own righteousness transforms one's humanity into the image and likeness of his and one is in heaven no longer the sinner one was except in memory.

Because the sin from which one is converted remains even as one is propelled out of bondage to it by way of a new relationship with God in Christ, the state of grace to which one is converted initiates no cumulative process either of simple, incremental improvement. The better one is by God's grace, the more serious one's continued failings become, the farther one has to fall in one's ongoing moral imperfection. One continues to confess one's sin not simply because one has not yet achieved enough in the effort to lead a reformed life but as a reminder of the simple sinner one remains apart from Christ, in recognition of one's utter dependence on Christ for all that one is that is good.

Conversion does not mean, then, being set on a new path oneself, absent one's former sins destroyed in Christ, being left with a now clean, blank slate to make the most of oneself through one's own renewed efforts to conform one's will with God. One's converted self does not, in other words, itself amount to a past to which one's future is chained in impossible expectation of perfection. It does not "create for the believer a life of obligation which must be persistently fulfilled" in the anxious effort to preserve the purity of one's initial converted state, at baptism for example.[26] One's baptism does not mean one's former sins are washed away so as to put one under the obligation of leading a blameless life thereafter, the grace of Christ in this way receding "behind the demand to fulfil the tasks which baptism imposes."[27] Such a demand would always be threatened by lapses into sin after baptism, requiring constant self-vigilance from the believer in either the futile attempt to prevent such lapses altogether or to atone for them subsequently. Postbaptismal sin would in this way bring one once again into God's debt, a debt to be forgiven by way of heartfelt confession and repentance, or to be remitted by virtue of one's compensatory future good deeds. The salvation that Christ brings would become in this way a kind of advance on what one is eventually to pay for oneself through holy living. God would become one's creditor again in Christ, loaning salvation on the expectation of being paid back by the good works that Christ makes possible.[28]

The language of debt and repayment can be appropriate for talking about the Christian response to postbaptismal sin, but in being so used it is shorn of most of its ordinary connotations.[29] Almsgiving, for example, is often talked about in the New Testament (and elsewhere) as a way of paying down debts owed to God because of sin; the debts of sin that might otherwise have prevented one's entrance into heaven are erased by the treasure

one banks there through gifts to the poor. Unlike ordinary repay-
ments of a debt, however, these payments are evidently not lost
to the borrower. What one apparently gives away to others in acts
of charity is transferred to one's own heavenly bank account, and
the interest received in exchange is exorbitant: salvation in exchange for often paltry sums. Moreover, repayment here redounds
to the benefit of the debtor rather than the creditor. God is not
temporarily bereft of what God has loaned out and therefore in
need of repayment; what one gives back to God is entered by God
into the borrower's own treasury in heaven.

But what most fundamentally disrupts the idea that one's
graced state poses an impossible demand on future conduct is
the fact that what one is indeed asked to achieve is already one's
own in Christ. Living in Christ, one is righteous because of
Christ's righteousness whatever one's own state. While certainly
to be struggled against, postbaptismal sin is also something to be
expected—one is saved while a sinner still. Postbaptismal sin, like
the sin that came before it, thereby loses its power to threaten
salvation that comes by way of life in Christ. One is united to
Christ and thus saved whatever the degree of one's continuing
sinfulness and despite sin's ongoing presence in one's life.

What God asks of us from the beginning may well be
impossible: perfect conformity with God's own will. One cannot hope to imitate the righteousness of God in one's deeds by
way of the created goods that constitute human life in and of
itself but only by way of God's own Spirit empowering one's
performance. Radical discontinuity may in that way exist between what we are given in the beginning and what we are to
achieve in the end, but God is the one who bridges the difference. God will supply the means to take us from the future
target, set for us in the past, to its eventual realization—not just
before baptism but after.

3

Total Commitment

The intense effort required by finance-dominated capitalism means little if corporations and creditors cannot find anyone willing to expend it. Making a deadline on time may require putting everything into meeting it at every waking moment. It may require maximum concentration and exertion, not just at work but at home, too. Servicing one's debt may require scrimping and saving on every item purchased and constant creativity in coming up with the necessary cash, turning every meager possession into a possible source of revenue, renting out one's already cramped space, finding buyers for unwanted junk, pawning what one would like to keep, selling one's food assistance coupons, and so on. But heightened demands like these are to no avail unless one can find people willing to comply with them. There is no point, for example, in a strategy of maximizing profit through work intensification if people are just not willing to work that hard; rather than increasing as intended, productivity will decline—difficult deadlines will simply go unmet.[1]

But what might bring people to commit themselves to such effort-filled exertions? Just because of the intensity of effort required, compliance with such demands cannot be presumed. Because so much is being asked of them, employees' cooperation, for example, certainly cannot be taken for granted. It becomes instead something that corporate management itself actively tries to promote.

Indeed, in service to a finance-backed interest in maximum profitability, corporations try to ensure not just maximum intensity of effort but maximum intensity of commitment to such effort.[2] Workers themselves are to want nothing more than what corporations ask of them; their own desires are to be brought into complete compliance with finance-dominated corporate interests, in order to increase productivity. Corporations expect maximum effort, while the only desire of their employees is to give it. By way of such a convergence, all critical distance on what finance-dominated capitalism requires from people disappears. How can one criticize what has become the desire of one's own heart?

Inducements to Comply with the Demand for Hard Work

Industrial capitalism typically induced hard work by compensating it. Employees are willing to do what they are asked to do in exchange for secure employment at good pay with benefits. Reneging on such commitments to workers becomes a recipe for labor unrest. Workers' commitment to the company is to be matched by the company's commitment to them. In exchange for hard work in the company's service, workers can expect to be employed for some time, promoted from within, and remunerated in ways that keep up with their contributions to what everyone has reason to hope will be an increasingly profitable enterprise.

Although some employees are paid handsomely in ways that align their own interests with corporate demands for maximum profitability (notably, CEOs who are paid in stock options), finance-dominated corporations typically cannot induce hard work in these ways. They downsize their labor forces whenever expedient in order to increase corporate profitability and are reluctant to share profits with their workers since any such sharing will have an immediate, adverse effect on profit margins. Instead, finance-dominated organizations use these very features of their management practices—their production of worker insecurity—to induce worker compliance through fear.

Where capitalism monopolizes the means to subsistence and there are no other viable ways of making a living, capitalism can always use fear to motivate worker compliance. One complies with what one's employer asks because one is afraid of the alternative—having one's pay docked or losing one's job. Finance-dominated capitalism ratchets up such fears by its usual management practices of maximizing profits through payroll cost-cutting. Every employee knows that he or she can be fired at some point or turned into some form of contingent worker at reduced pay and benefits. Employees come and go all the time, and such contingent employees—part-timers, independent contractors, and full-time temps—are often one's coworkers. The implied threat is therefore always quite salient. Moreover, the penalties for failure to comply under finance-dominated capitalism become more extreme. Austerity measures enforced by international holders of national debt hollow out welfare provisions: losing one's job could very well mean living on the street, chronically hungry and exposed to the elements, like the poor people one passes everyday on the way to and from work. Being fired would not be so bad if one could easily find another permanent position appropriate to one's skills, at equal or better pay. But the downward pressures on employment in finance-dominated capitalism make that a very uncertain prospect. Where downsizing is a general corporate strategy, such hopes reasonably dwindle. Whatever one's skill level or previous work experience, one might legitimately fear enlistment in the growing ranks of poorly paid temps or service workers.

Compliance out of fear is not, however, optimal from the profit-maximizing viewpoint of finance-dominated capitalism because it brings with it no guarantee of effectiveness, in and of itself. While one complies willingly, conformity with the wishes of finance-dominated capitalism out of fear suggests some reluctance. Other things being equal, one might very well prefer not to; in doing one's job, one is very possibly acting against what one would otherwise freely choose to do, that is, in the absence of the constraints posed by the need for employment. Although voluntary, performing as one is asked would therefore be something like throwing cargo overboard in the effort to keep one's ship afloat in a storm or handing over one's wallet to an armed gunman—necessary when under threat but something one would very much like to avoid, and therefore what one might be actively inclined to shirk or escape entirely if given the opportunity. When induced by fear, compliance can be assured, then, only under conditions of constant work surveillance, thereby adding monitoring costs to the usual labor expenses of corporations.

Aside from the one-time cost of setting them up, such surveillance can be done quite cheaply—at little ongoing expense—through the use of computerized technologies, with the ability, for example, to count every keystroke and continually track reaction times. Surveillance tasks can also be delegated to employees themselves without adding further layers of management. Peer-group pressure within a team framework has this effect. Strict canons of self-auditing can also be mandated, although the time and effort required to do that auditing itself cuts down on worker productivity and is arguably always less than effective because it is left at least partially to the discretion of potentially disgruntled employees. Continual assessment, especially when it has the capacity to pinpoint individual performance, has the advantage, however, of further instilling fear: there is nowhere to hide, no possibility of escape at work; slacking off and poor performance will always be noticed and punished.

Similar problems of assuring compliance beset the use of external rewards to induce effort. Employees are willing to do what is asked of them for instrumental reasons, because the pay they receive can be used to obtain outside of work what they primarily want and desire. Employees are willing to put up with tasks they would otherwise prefer not to perform because of what their wages will get them—the consumer goods that promise to satisfy both basic needs and desires for fulfillment that fundamentally have nothing to do with work. Like fear, the "I'd otherwise prefer not to" character of a utilitarian approach to work brings with it the same monitoring costs. Without continual supervision, it is impossible to be sure that workers are in fact doing what they are being asked to do. Efforts to maximize profit by payroll cost-cutting also work against the success of such inducements: employees are not being paid enough to make all this effort on the job worth their while, and the goods that might compensate them for their efforts become too expensive to buy. One might also suspect—in line with Daniel Bell's famous argument in *The Cultural Contradictions of Capitalism*—that compliance with corporate demands for utilitarian reasons is constantly being undermined by the contrary character of the pursuit of consumer goods that is supposed to motivate it.[3] Because the work one does is not intrinsically satisfying, a utilitarian approach to work for the sake of external reward presumes the ability to defer gratification: one has to learn to wait until one is paid and can go out and buy what brings enjoyment after all the work is done. A consumer mentality, by contrast, encourages the pursuit of immediate gratification: buy it now, enjoy it now, be happy at once. At work one submits, however grudgingly, to the demands of others, while at the store one is encouraged to revel in the free play of impulse.

The threat to productivity and profit posed by the mismatch between what workers left to their own devices would prefer to be doing and what the company is asking them to do at work can be circumvented in a couple of ways, both increasingly common within finance-dominated capitalism. Rather than struggle to bring the always potentially recalcitrant desires of workers into line with company mandates, companies can institute work processes that have the effect, at least at work, of evacuating all such potentially contrary impulses and desires from workers' minds. This can be done through the sort of tight-flow production processes outlined in the last chapter.[4] An employee's task has to be addressed right away and is so difficult to perform in the time allowed that it requires one's complete attention. No time for daydreaming, then, about what one would rather be doing or the pleasures that might await one after work. If the task is to be completed to company specifications, one must be entirely absorbed in its performance.

An even more extreme form of self-evacuation occurs in work processes that promote and enforce a near machinic reactivity.[5] The work at hand pushes out not just thought of anything else but thought per se. Reflection would inhibit performance of the task at hand, which requires one simply to react as quickly as possible in the appropriately scripted way to the changing stimuli of inputs that constantly come one's way. Call centers are a good example.[6] Computerized technologies distribute tasks to workers with maximum efficiency—as soon as one call ends another comes in. The speed of one's reaction time is continuously being monitored, as is the length of time one takes to respond to customer queries, which means optimally without deviation from the pre-established script that fits the particular sort of question one is being asked. Workers become nothing more than a kind of blank interface or surface of contact where customer and service provision meet; thought is no more relevant here than it is in response to an ATM's request for one's PIN or one's car's "request," by losing speed, for more pressure on the gas pedal. The inputs one is being given are mere signals, refusing all further interpretation or thought.

Financial trading, especially where the appropriate reaction to rapidly changing market conditions is determined by formulas or computerized programming, has much the same machinic qualities. Response to market stimuli needs to be as automatic as possible in as highly disciplined a way as possible. One must be practiced in winnowing down one's mental life to what is simply required for an immediate reaction in keeping with what the computer models say the particular market stimuli at hand call for. Which means one should winnow one's mental life down to next to nothing. Thinking too much, second guessing, simply means that the opportunities available at the moment will have passed one by. Thinking about what current market trends might mean—for one's financial well-being or the future of one's wife and children or one's prospects for happiness—at best simply slows down reaction time; at worst, it threatens to interfere with the appropriate response according to computerized models. So, for example, needing an influx of cash at once to pay one's child's college tuition, a day trader might hold a stock longer than one should in hopes of further price increases beyond the point at which the computer model tells one to sell. Over the course of the multiple trades that make up one's day, one thereby loses one's shirt, punished by the market for deviance from established protocols in as harsh a manner as any meted out by a call center supervisor with the power to dock one's pay in proportion to the decline in the number of calls completed over the course of a day.[7]

Like at a call center, discipline in conformity comes about here by way of a certain kind of self-renunciation. One does not conform by struggling to bring one's own will into line with a superior will or market demand. The latter is simply to replace one's own will; it becomes, for all intents and purposes at work, the only will one has.

But the major way that finance-dominated capitalism deals with the lurking threat to productivity and profit of any disparity between what workers want and what companies want from them is simply to do everything possible to close the gap. Workers are to be encouraged to want for themselves what the company wants from them. Ideally, the two sets of desires should be brought into complete alignment.[8] Were such a convergence to be achieved, workers would never be acting reluctantly, simply because they want to get something else by way of that compliance or to avoid unpleasant penalties for failing to do so. Working in the way the company wants would be instead the primary object of one's own desires, in and of itself the primary means of satisfying them.

Since workers would only be doing as they like in comply-
ing with company dictates, secondary measures to assure that
compliance—such as monitoring costs—could ideally be cut
to the bone. Workers would monitor themselves, not by way of
some after-the-fact self-audit, cutting into time and energy to
be devoted to the primary business of the day, but simply in
the natural course of conforming their actions to their own
will, in the natural course of carrying out their own intentions.
And rather than struggling to turn human beings into machine-
like, thoughtlessly reactive automatons—through work processes that encourage practices of self-evacuation and self-
renunciation—companies could leave workers alone to do as
the workers see fit. The companies could grant workers the
autonomy of their own self-directed actions, as post-Fordist
forms of work organization seem to favor.

Finding value in the work one is asked to do is something
that the old Protestant work ethic supplied. One could count
on the hard work of employees because they found satisfaction
themselves in doing so. Workers who work for work's sake are
not, however, especially self-directing; they need to be told what
to do, thereby incurring a host of managerial costs. The Protestant work ethic is no doubt in part for this reason associated
with the unadventurously obedient "company man" within
highly developed bureaucracies that effectively transfer direction in step-by-step fashion down from the top. Workers conforming to a Protestant work ethic can take pleasure in the
successful performance of whatever it is they have been told to
do; they take a certain pleasure in following the lead of others,
the satisfaction from doing so following closely upon and remaining internal to conformity with company demands at work.
Finance-dominated corporations save on costs of both monitoring and directing employees by requiring them instead to

take responsibility themselves for decision-making (within parameters set by top management). They are to be self-moving, taking the initiative to deal effectively with the changing demands of a fast-paced market. Self-generated initiative of that sort is necessary to take maximum advantage of whatever the market throws at one; it is a function, in other words, of the flexibility in task performance demanded by a changing marketplace (and the concomitant post-Fordist desire to avoid all immobile sunk costs, whether in equipment or human capital).

Finally, the Protestant work ethic is as vulnerable as any inducement to hard work that involves both overt submission to the will of others and deferred gratification. Waiting patiently for the rewards of hard work at work—incremental pay raises and promotions over the course of a long career that loyal submission to one's employer brings—seems at cross-purposes with the life one is encouraged to lead outside work through the constant lure of easy credit and incessant advertising. Rather than delaying, one can get whatever one wants or needs now by borrowing. The long, hard work of paying off such loans becomes a dim prospect rather than a necessary prerequisite for satisfying pressing desires of the moment.

Under finance-dominated capitalism, the character of pursuit of one's desires, whether at work or outside of it, is taken to be much the same.[9] One is to relate to oneself in uniform fashion, whatever the context. Encouraged to see life both at work and outside of it in much the same terms, the latter loses its potential to undermine the former. Both are arguably reconceived in the process, so that they converge not only with one another but, perhaps more importantly, with finance-dominated corporate interests in maximum profitability.

Whether at home, at the store, or at work, one should be the sort of person who assumes responsibility for making the most of what one has in pursuit of one's goals: the ever greater achievement of self-realization and self-fulfillment. Put into more financialized terms (this is arguably indeed just a general cultural trend since the 1960s coopted for finance-dominated purposes), one should make every effort, in a self-directed way, to maximize the profitable employment of the assets one has in one's person. Whether rich or poor, one has certain God-given talents; one can, in any case, aspire to acquire more lucrative capabilities through further education and training. All such assembled personal assets are to be put to maximally efficient use for the greatest possible profit in one's person, to maximize personal growth, to produce an ever-increasing gross domestic product in one's person.

One can exhibit this same sort of attitude toward oneself throughout the course of one's whole life—in preparing for adulthood, in the choice of a spouse and the running of a household, in every consumer purchase, in taking out loans to further such purchases or finance extended education or training—as well as at work. In each and every case, one assumes responsibility for enhancing the value of one's assets and putting them to work for one's own benefit in the most profitable possible fashion at the lowest possible expense. An ongoing effort to enhance the value of personal assets and put them to work in the pursuit of self-fulfillment in this way comes to cover every dimension of life: "Continuously engaged in a project to shape his or her life as an autonomous choosing individual driven by the desire to optimize the worth of his or her own existence, life for that person [becomes] a single basically undifferentiated arena for the pursuit of that endeavor."[10] Gone are any arenas of life requiring from one any fundamentally different self-understanding and capable thereby of calling such a self-understanding into question.[11]

More than understanding one's life to require the efficient use of scarce resources in a self-interested pursuit of personal preferences—more than considering oneself a *Homo economicus*—here one considers one's very self, one's very person, to be a kind of economic property whose value is to be maximized by highly efficient employment, by increasing productivity in one's labor on it.[12] One is not simply considering in economic terms the pursuit of whatever preferences one happens to have but considering oneself to be an economic resource upon which to capitalize. One's self is what one works on; one's self is what one adds value to by way of such self-directed labor.

It has not been unusual since the early days of capitalism to think of having property in one's person. The labor power one owns in virtue of that fact can be exchanged for wages in an employment contract. Property in one's person amounts to a kind of private property. One can do what one likes with private property, loaning it out for a time, as one does with one's labor power, and assuming the proceeds received in exchange; one has the right to keep others from any unremunerated use or appropriation of it, and so on. Under finance-dominated capitalism, the idea of having property in one's person takes the more specific form of capital; that is, property in one's person becomes an asset to be used to generate further profit, with the proceeds (or losses) of such use returning to the owner.

One takes up, in short, a peculiar sort of business relationship with oneself. It is a business model that is being extended here to cover all dimensions of life, so as to draw one's self-understanding into increasing alignment with how actual businesses are run in finance-dominated capitalism. Like the owner of a business, one has certain sunk costs that represent investments in oneself; one makes such investments in hopes of turning a profit but at considerable risk and with no guarantees. In order to make that profit, what could be more reasonable than turning on oneself the maximizing posture of actual corporations, disciplined by finance? Why make a little when one could make a lot? The pressures on profitability that one faces as an individual are much the same, indeed, as those faced by actual corporations: pressures posed by debt and the constant need to retool to reflect changing market conditions. Corporate America would seem to provide appropriate models for meeting such challenges in one's own life. It is in one's own interest, for example, to keep investments in the capital assets of one's person mobile and flexible (just as corporations try to do with equipment and personnel), since one never knows when the particular skills one has will become obsolete. Perhaps it is also in one's own interest in fulfilling oneself to demand almost more from oneself than one could ever deliver, to work harder and harder, to the point of near exhaustion, in an attempt to increase one's own worth to the maximum.

Whether one ever starts up a business or not, one can run one's life like an entrepreneur, both owning and managing the assets of one's life for profit-maximizing purposes, taking the initiative to make the most of all available opportunities, showing the resourcefulness to make do oneself with what one has rather than depending on others to make one's way in the world. Although corporations are typically not owned and managed by a single person—by an actual entrepreneur—they are typically now understood in the same terms, as exhibiting the same sort of entrepreneurial spirit.[13]

Taking on such a relationship with oneself becomes all the more unquestionable as a business model like this extends over every sort of organized, institutionalized activity within finance-dominated capitalism. Government offices are increasingly run in the same way, as if they were private businesses charged with delivering services as cheaply and efficiently as possible, even if that means downsizing and underpaying the workforce and severely curtailing any such services.[14] Institutions of higher learning are also coming to be managed in much the same way, with a primary concern for increased returns on assets. Student customers are lured by "value for money," which is achieved by way of budget cutting and poorly paid adjunct labor, thus becoming almost a training ground for a corporate mentality of profit maximization.[15]

The upshot of all this for the employment relationship is to bring the self-understanding of employees into perfect alignment with the self-understanding of the firm employing them. One's own self-understanding becomes no different from that of one's employer: I am a business; the firm I work for is a business just like me, managing its assets in the same way I do in the attempt to assure maximum profitability. Indeed, my understanding of myself is identical with my employer's view of me, because we are both making use of the very same assets in our respective business ventures. The company I work for is a business trying to maximize its profits by the way I am put to work. I am trying to maximize the return on those same assets in my person by putting myself to work using much the same techniques (not just at work but everywhere else) as a form of self-management. My employer considers me human capital to be put to maximally profitable use at the least expense, and that is also how I see myself: my personal assets are my own human capital in the running of what I hope will be the enormously profitable business of my own life. It is hard therefore to criticize my employer for seeing me that way. In each case the assets of my person are being put to work in a manner designed to produce maximum profit; that simply seems to be what they are for.

Of course, the maximally profitable use of my human capital by the firm I work for might not be maximally profitable for me, producing in me a certain reluctance, even resistance, to being so used. Why think the corporation's efforts to capitalize on my assets will not come at the expense of my own efforts? If one is simply thinking in monetary terms, that often seems in fact to be the case: corporate revenues and profit margins go up without being shared proportionately with employees in the form of increased wages and benefits. But one does not have to be well remunerated for one's human capital to be enhanced through work and rendered profitable for oneself. Multiskilling has that effect, for instance: the ability to perform the variety of quite different tasks one is asked to do at work— use the machine, fix the machine, change its fittings, use it to make different things, and so on—enhances one's human capital in the form of greater employability. If (and when) one is let go, one stands a greater chance of being rehired. Work enhances one's capacities in a way one can keep wherever one goes.

But more generally, management practices that allow employees to be self-directing in keeping with their own talents are in effect promising to maximize corporate profits only by way of employees' own efforts to maximize their human capital for their own purposes. The corporation stands to profit only if workers do since it is only in and through the value-enhancing self-management practices of employees that profit for the corporation is generated to begin with. Such corporations give every impression of having an interest in the self-realization of their employees in and through the work those employees perform. For example, while they may not pay for the training necessary to perform required tasks well, or provide it in-house (since that raises expenses), they may give employees every opportunity to practice better self-management in the exercise of such skills—by assigning specific projects to particular work teams who are to assume responsibility themselves for figuring out how to carry them out expeditiously, at the least possible cost, and with often minimal resources with which to work. It is only because of the efficiencies and the defraying of layer upon layer of management costs, which such resourceful employee self-direction brings, that the company is able to maximize its own profits. Just to the extent corporations do have this sort of interest themselves in an employee's growing self-management skills, rather than being simply an overworked and hard-pressed employee, one can consider oneself to be running one's own little business within a business that will not profit unless the employee does. If one fails in one's efforts to enhance one's human capital in and through the work one performs, one's profit-generating capacities for the corporation will decline as well.

Corporations have such an interest in fostering employees' sense of self-realization through work, not simply because it makes them more efficient and lowers costs but because it cements their commitment to their work. A company can trust such employees to be totally invested in their work and therefore to give it their all. Commitment to work when it figures significantly in one's life project as an entrepreneurial self is no superficial commitment, a mere surface sham or show, but something lodged in one's person, a part of who one is. Personal commitment of that kind brings with it an unreserved, no-holds-barred commitment to the hard work companies demand.

Looking for such commitment in hiring decisions, company attention therefore centers on the character of one's person rather than on one's technical skills. Technical skills have little weight in hiring decisions where the positions to be filled no longer involve fixed tasks according to well-defined job specifications. Instead, a typical company tries to determine whether one is the sort of person inclined and capable of expanding one's skill set, at one's own initiative (and expense), in the attempt to improve performance of complex tasks. In hiring someone, a company is, in short, no longer simply trying to enlist a particular form of one's labor power but attempting to put the whole of one's capabilities on call.[16]

Even when particular qualifications for the job are at issue, employers remain preoccupied with a person's character. They are not simply interested in whether one can do the job given one's current skill set, but in the attitudes one has with respect to work. Does one enjoy and find fulfillment in one's work? How central is it to one's life? Does one, for example, have family obligations that might draw one's energies away from work or outside hobbies that might align one with it, an avid skier to be tasked with selling ski equipment? How resourceful and energetic is one likely to be in applying one's skills to the task at hand? One must have the knowhow, the qualifications to perform the job, but one must also have the requisite "knowhow-to-be; that is, the [right] behavior and attitude regarding work, the environment (for example, the supervisory staff, colleagues, company), and vis-à-vis oneself (do you want to progress?)."[17] As much as job performance, character, and fundamental disposition are primary matters for employer concern. The demands of the job are not to insert themselves simply at the level of temporarily induced behavior while on the job, leaving one's person alone—to daydream during its performance or, if that's not possible, to pursue other modes of living outside of it. One's very person, at the level of its most fundamental projects, is to become the insertion point for company profit-taking; every employee must have an entrepreneurial self, relating to oneself as an enterprise for profit, if the company itself is to be profitable in the optimal way that finance demands. People are hired because they think of themselves that way and remain on staff to the extent they can demonstrate as much in the way they apply themselves to work.

Of course it is often hard to know for certain whether employees are really giving it their all, whether they are actually working at full capacity with total commitment to successful performance, if they are genuinely working at their own discretion. Especially when tasks are complex and require teamwork, individual effort is hard to quantify and therefore tends to escape even the best low-cost computerized surveillance systems. This is indeed one reason for the shift of employer concern to the personal characters of employees. Difficulty in monitoring behaviors of self-managing workers means that their basic attitudes and intentions with respect to work become all the more important. An employer has to count on their being the sort of people who habitually and as a matter of principle give work their all, the sort of people who make it their own business (in a quite literal sense) to make creative use of all opportunities offered for innovative improvements in productive processes, maximally efficient use of all available resources, however meager, and so on. But how to be sure of any of that apart from the character of their actual work performances? Interior dispositions, one's fundamental intentions and desires, are even harder to monitor than outward behaviors. Am I really committed to wanting what my employer wants from me or merely faking it? Are such desires authentically mine—my own self-generated desires—or simply feigned to meet what remains an external demand to show such commitment? In light of reasonable fears like these, employer confidence in one's commitment to work needs to be constantly shored up, constantly reassured, by signs, witnesses, and testimony to one's utter and wholehearted commitment: cars left in the parking lot all night, a change of clothes in one's office drawers, the empty food cartons that show one has eaten every meal of the day at one's desk, attendance at all "optional" employment gatherings, however they might infringe on time with one's family, and so on.[18] Like a seventeenth-century penitent, one must not only express regret for any lapse in performance—act contrite—but also display one's tears, a more heartfelt attrition in keeping with genuine love for any requests that have gone unfulfilled.[19] By all such means, one attempts to prove not just that one's own desires are to work in the way one is asked but that one is fully committed to those desires in a wholehearted fashion that brooks no opposition or divided loyalties.

The very fact, however, that company profit comes by way of my own self-fulfillment at work may lead me to question how genuine is company interest in it. While the company may constantly question the degree to which I genuinely love my work, it is equally hard to still suspicions about company intentions with respect to me. My work on myself is quite obviously being instrumentalized by the company as a means to its own ends of maximum profit. Treated as a means rather than an end, why should I not suspect that the company's supposed respect for my qualities as a person and for my resourceful self-directing capacities as an agent is itself a mere sham and superficial show?[20] Is the company genuinely interested, for example, in what makes me the irreplaceably specific person I am or just in the completely fungible, general capacity I have to be molded in whatever way it sees fit?[21] Such suspicions are only heightened by the also very obvious fact that my commitment to my work will never be matched by the commitment of the company to me. However committed I may be to my work, the company is always more than willing simply to use me up and throw me away whenever that seems expedient.

Moreover, the more the demand for commitment to work is totalized, the harder it becomes to see it as anything more than an unduly restrictive narrowing of one's own entrepreneurial life project. Making lovely widgets might be part of such a life project but one does not only want to want what one's employer wants from one; it is hard to see the desire to make those widgets as the whole of one's heart's desires. One has much larger life objectives that exceed the constricted range of company objectives and that therefore butt up against the demand for total commitment to them. It is the narrow fixing of objectives by work, in other words, rather than simple alienation from work—which one remains in fact committed to—that provides a constant source of possible disgruntlement.[22]

The company can be kept from being the target of this potential disgruntlement, and even the feeling itself stilled, the more both worker and employer seem at the mercy of wider forces beyond their control. The market, an inexorable and diffuse force, is calling the shots; the company, along with its workers, has no choice but to follow the market's lead if any profits are to be had by anyone. What the company demands from workers represents no deliberate choice of an optional course by company management but simply what the market itself requires. Unlike a company managed by actual people at a head office, an impersonal market is implacable, and its source of direction without apparent location.

It is not simply that market conditions—say, increased competition from overseas companies with cheap labor costs—make these management decisions the only viable ones. The strong impression is given that the market itself is managing the corporation. Rather than being the ultimate source of the free decision to manage workers in this particular way, the company is only following in an almost reactive way the market's own dictates. If the price of the company's stock falls, layoffs ensue. If orders slow by a certain percentage in a particular week, the next week sees a proportionate drop in the hours that employees will be asked to work. Whether one is asked to work and what one is asked to do simply mirror the ups and downs, the changing character, of the market itself. Market mediation seems, in other words, to replace for all intents and purposes in-house corporate deliberation about worker management. When it comes to labor policies, corporations let the market make the decisions for them. Rather than setting wage rates in-house, for example, companies leave the decision about what to pay one's workers to the market: the market sets the going rate for janitorial services, and one naturally hires the company that will provide such services at the lowest price. If one does not like management policies like these—how workers are paid, the way their work schedules are set, the time pressures, the changing work assignments—complain to the market and see how far that goes.

The only arena of freedom left to workers would seem to lie in the attitude they choose to assume toward being managed by the market. The only thing they can do anything about, the only matter that remains under their control, is how they take the fact of their lives being so determined. Their working lives will conform to market dictates whether they like it or not; they can either do so willingly and come to desire themselves what is an inevitability in any case, as the company would like, or doom themselves to aimless, untargeted dissatisfaction without hope of relief. Is there any real choice to be made here?[23]

Mirroring the market, and taking satisfaction in that fact, one comes to completely identify oneself with it. I am the market, as successful investment bankers and traders in financial assets so often say.[24] One can understand one's life projects to be entirely incorporated within the life of the market, one aspect of its own ongoing, overarching processes. I no longer work on myself, then, simply for the sake of myself, but for something much bigger than I am and bigger than any company I work for. I am driven beyond self-preoccupation by self-identification with the market itself, driven beyond myself in ways that only bring me into closer alignment with market forces. For all my self-initiated self-management, I am self-evacuated, as much as any call center operator, of anything beyond what the market dictates, so that the market seems to be extending its own life in and through me.

Finance-dominated corporations typically combine all these ways of inducing unswerving conformity from employees: they use techniques of fear, love, and self-evacuation to bring about compliance. Self-managing employees, for example, are not usually left unsupervised but are often heavily monitored as if they were not to be trusted. They give their all not just because they find fulfillment in such work but because they fear losing their jobs. And once they enter the flow of work demands, that flow often takes on a life of its own and seems to carry them along whether they like it or not, as if what was happening were all taking place apart from their own doing or willing of it.[25] Corporations no doubt combine such techniques with the expectation that they will prove mutually reinforcing. In case exhaustion makes me question the intrinsic value to me of what I am doing—whether I am really finding self-fulfillment in working so hard both day and night—fear of demotion or job loss can step into the breach.

On the other hand, the combination can make for an uneasy alliance. If my employer really has an interest in the free exercise of my creative agency—because the company's own ends are achieved only by giving me free rein—why am I being constantly monitored at every step to make sure everything I do in fact serves company ends? Isn't corporate respect for my individual autonomy clearly limited, given those facts? If my own desires are really in perfect sync with those of my employer, why do I find a gun at my head? I am well aware that any failure in showing myself to be fully committed to my work could bring the hammer down at any time. As Frédéric Lordon suggests, "The failure to induce [my own] desire, the imperfect adaptation, and the incomplete accommodation, at once bring back the iron fist of the employment relation, whether in the form of downward social mobility, demotion-reassignment, or, finally, pure and simple dismissal."[26] The lingering threat hanging over all that I do can only make me question the degree to which my own desires are what is really motivating me. Am I personally committed or merely obeying an external command? Doesn't a demand for personal commitment, the company ultimatum to display it, simply compromise it? For all my personal investment, demonstrated by resourcefulness in the skillful managing of my own aptitudes at work, how different am I from a retail worker or service provider forced to smile and be pleasant to customers, under conditions of constant surveillance and the threat of immediate job loss? How deep does my enjoyment of what I am being asked to do really go?

Christian Commitment to God

Christianity can enter here to help drive a wedge between my desires and the company's, interrupting the mechanisms for gaining the sort of total commitment required for maximum corporate profitability. Commitment to God and the conversion that brings it about interfere with total commitment to anything else, thereby limiting the degree to which I could ever be completely personally invested in a company's aims.

Commitment to God gains such a capacity, ironically, to the extent it amounts itself to a life project with certain similarities to the enterprise self of finance-dominated capitalism. One should seize every opportunity, at every moment, over the course of one's entire life to become a person oriented to God. All that one is and everything one experiences should be considered the raw material for one's spiritual progress, the constant occasion for work on oneself that would draw one nearer to God in thanks and praise, and into greater alignment with God's will for the world.[27]

Christianity is to promote, in short, a form of work on oneself in which one problematizes one's own piety with a maximizing intent: one is to make an issue of one's own religiousness in ways that turn that religiousness itself into a maximizing project. One should be as religious as possible in the sense of directing oneself to God in thanks and praise and into alignment with God's will at every moment and in everything one does.[28]

In so doing, the formation of one's self-understanding as a Christian, how one relates to oneself as a Christian, turns into an ongoing life task determinative of one's entire person, making one simply the person one is. Living life Christianly comes to form the core of one's identity, something to which one is wholeheartedly committed in the sense that, were one no longer engaged in such a project, one would no longer be the person one is.

Orientation of oneself to God becomes so wholehearted just to the extent one's Christian commitments become both all-encompassing and capable of unifying, bringing together, every other desire one has. Unlike devotion to deities in Greco-Roman religion, with its circumscribed functions of, for example, protecting the city from harm, and more like the entire person-forming capacity of an ancient philosophy, Christian commitment to God is not to be exhibited in only those spheres of life specifically dedicated to it but should make itself felt throughout the whole of one's life.[29] No mere matter for intermittent consideration, depending on the character of the setting or circumstances, such commitment should become the constant focal point of one's life direction; never neglected, such a commitment is to be activated, actively engaged, at every moment without fail.[30] One must be constantly asking whether, and if so how, all of one's other pursuits fit into one's primary Christian commitment. By in some way appearing in everything else one goes on to do, Christian commitment would become incorporative of every other more mundane desire, bending all such aims under its own purposes.

The general mechanisms employed within Christianity to assure wholehearted commitment to God run radically contrary, however, to those used by finance-dominated capitalism to induce total compliance. In keeping with the way God works God's own will in the world, such commitment is not, first of all, to be brought about by way of self-evacuation. God works God's will by way of my own will, not by substituting for it. Whatever my will is, even if that will is consciously opposed to God's own intentions, God can work God's will in and through it. The prototypical example would be the cross; God fulfills God's purposes to save through the very human repudiation of those efforts. But in making a commitment to God, my aim is to bring what remains my own will into deliberate correspondence with God's (to the extent I am ever able to know it). That requires no simple repudiation of my own will for fulfillment since I can be confident in Christ that God's will is also for my own good. God's desire is to save me.

Conversion does involve the repudiation of what I have been—the sinner I am—but that sort of self-refusal or break with myself need not translate into self-evacuation before God, or before anyone else.[31] Dying to my old life of sin requires not the death of my will per se and its replacement by another—by God's will or that of my religious superior—so that the latter is the only will I am to have, but the turning around of my own will, the reversing of its direction. A will turned away from God is now, by virtue of my new life in Christ, to be turned toward God. All that is to be put to death is the will's sinful orientation.

Commitment to God by way of such a conversion does, however, complicate the integration of my ordinary commitments into it; the two can never completely coincide in the way a company expects the aims of a worker to coincide with its own. Insofar as conversion continues into the present as an ongoing state of breaking with one's past, because sin is no over-and-done-with moment relegated to the past but always remains to be turned away from, every single present project of mine is to be repudiated to some extent or other (some of them more than others)—just to the extent such a project becomes a sinful interference to wholehearted orientation to God and God's will for the world. Indeed, making one's ordinary investments wholehearted—which is to say excluding God from them—is often how such interference comes about. That very sort of investment in the ordinary is what Christians should be actively turning away from in the continual process of conversion with which Christians are tasked.

Conversion, in short, requires a certain fundamental form of disinvestment in the ordinary pursuit of one's mundane desires. One should never be wholeheartedly committed to any ordinary pursuit in the way one is to be committed to God. Full commitment to God does bring with it a commitment to all the things that God is committed to—including one's own good, care for the unfortunate, and so on. But the effort to be committed to anything else in that same wholehearted way will exclude God in a sinful distortion of one's dependence on God for any furtherance of even those this-worldly aims ordained by God.

Indeed, simply the overarching, comprehensive character of commitment to God encourages disinvestment in every other project or the totality of them. One can pursue a commitment to God in and through every other commitment one has (although how one does so may take very different forms). For that reason none of them is of any irreplaceable significance. No particular task or life project has a monopoly in supplying occasions for orienting oneself to God and God's will. One can orient oneself to God, try to bring oneself into greater alignment with God's will, whatever the circumstances, whatever one's job, whatever the tasks one has been saddled with.

The specific form that orientation to God takes may vary with circumstances, but the intensity of God-directed focus can (and should) continue with the same constancy across them all. The good that one does for oneself and others, the good that one experiences oneself from others, can easily become, for example, the occasion for praise and rejoicing in God's beneficence. The harm that one does to others can become the material for equally intense Godward self-direction in the form of confession, contrition, and repentance, and the ultimate effort to turn away from such behaviors. And the harm one is suffering at the hands of others might issue in heartfelt pleas for divine aid to get one out of it, if that be God's will.

Because it runs across all the different pursuits in which one might be engaged, a Christian life project has the capacity to reinforce the distance from roles and tasks that is typical of modernity and that finance-dominated capitalism attempts to close up with its demands for total commitment. Enabled by the sociocultural differentiation of modern life, mobility, whether real or imagined, keeps one from identifying with any particular role or task in ways that would heavily invest one in its performance. One can assume one social role or occupational task and then another across the course of one's lifetime: one can start out a poor man and end up a rich one, begin one's employment as a baker and move on to construction work. The norms that guide action become differentiated according to the sphere of life they cover, so that on any one day, one behaves quite differently at work than one does at home, differently at church than when training in one's capacity as an army reservist, and so forth. In the absence of actual mobility across such spheres, one can at least imagine oneself living quite differently, assuming quite different roles and behaviors from those that therefore merely happen to define one's life. Interdependence among specialized occupations and social functions encourages a recognition of non-discounted differences. One can imagine oneself doing what others do, because one's dependence on their relatively autonomous activity makes it harder to see their differences from one as a function of insanity or subhumanity or their unfortunate placement on some lower rung of sociocultural development on the way to one's own—as simply a matter, in short, of error, immorality, or immaturity. Because one does many different things oneself, assumes many different roles in a variety of social spheres—or can at least imagine oneself doing so—no one such form of action or manner of living captures who one is as a person. One distinguishes one's self from any and all of that; one relates to oneself in ways that assume a certain distance from all one's social roles and tasks. A certain level of disinvestment in them comes about because one no longer identifies oneself with them.

Insofar as a Christian life project is to be carried across any and all of one's other pursuits, it encourages a similar sort of imagined mobility, with similar effects: it dovetails with and enhances the distancing from any particular social role and occupational task that is a function of mobility in modernity. One's Christian identity does not require one to assume any other socially defined role or task; the Christian stakes in any particular person-defining social role are quite low. For that reason, the task of orienting oneself to God that makes up one's Christian identity is never collapsible into any one, or even the totality, of such social roles. Instead, it is to follow one across every different role and task one might be asked to perform; one is tasked with imagining how one might live out one's Christian identity in any and all of them. The Christian self-project is not itself therefore one among the other ordinary tasks and roles one could inhabit. It is related to those other roles and tasks in the irreducible way one's person is, according to a modern self-understanding.

Because it does not sit alongside those positions as something like a social role or peculiar occupational task in its own right, one's Christian identity need not simply substitute itself for the other identities one assumes in the course of other pursuits. It incorporates them, instead, in a critical, relativizing fashion. One in some sense remains what one is in virtue of the various roles and tasks one undertakes—a once baker, now construction worker in the national guard who attends church regularly—but these identities are reworked (to varying degrees) within a project of God orientation to provide one with a new identity in and through them. They all become the mere matter given form in Christ and are in that sense overridden or written over.

As the particular person one is, one's life takes on the character of Christ's: one's life turns into the project of leading a God-directed life as his was, by virtue of the power of Christ's Spirit within one providing the principle for one's thorough-going self-reformation. Despite sharing such a project with others and therefore assuming a common identity with them in Christ, one retains one's particular identity: one is just this particular person, as that is established by one's having assumed just this combination of mundane roles and tasks, leading such a life project of God orientation. But in its capacity to encompass and reform all the others, one's identity in Christ becomes one's primary one. Everything else that I have become as the particular person I am is seen through Christ, and only in that way am I justified and sanctified. God's judgment on my sin is averted and forgiveness gained, for example, because the identity I have in Christ trumps what I have otherwise made of myself. Sanctified already in that identification with Christ's holiness overrules my own continued sinfulness, I show the primacy of that identity in Christ by constant efforts at complete self-reform.

Finance-dominated capitalism, by insisting on role and task flexibility in the pursuit of maximum profit, also encourages a form of self-understanding that distinguishes one's person from the tasks one assumes. One should identify oneself with one's capacities to perform a variety of tasks and do everything one can to enhance such capacities; that is the all-encompassing task that distinguishes one's person from anything in particular one does. The point of such enhancement, however, is simply to enable one to immerse oneself completely in whatever task one is asked to perform and then to go on to the next, with the same readiness for total engagement. Identifying oneself with one's capacities is what makes one, in short, perfectly malleable to company demands. It becomes thereby a way of denying (rather than assuring) the irreducible particularity of employees as persons. Since everyone is to be similarly capacitated, one person becomes interchangeable with every other. No one is irreplaceable: if one is for some reason unable to perform (because one's child is sick) or simply unwilling (because one is fed up), someone else is always available to take one's place.

Christianity also enjoins a peculiar sort of malleability, the capacity to make oneself over, the ultimate end being conformity with God. And Christianity calls one to identify oneself with that capacity: one is created in the image of God because, unlike other creatures, one has the oddly open capacity to become not simply an excellent human being but something like God, who is wholly different from any of God's creatures.[32] Because, however, of the way one's identity in Christ comprehensively reworks all of one's other identities, valuing this sort of malleability does not mean valuing one's interchangeable capacity to perform the very same tasks that others do. Nor for the same reason does valuing malleability entail valuing one's ability to make over all other tasks and projects in a homogenizing way. That identity does not erase the differences among spheres in the way the single, normative frame of asset maximization does; one does not increase capacities for God direction simply by collapsing every other project into it and replacing every other normative frame with its own—in the way, say, norms of public service are replaced by profit maximizing ones once an enterprise self becomes one's unifying, all-encompassing identity.

Because it is capable of being pursued across every other enterprise, an orientation to God takes on money's character of putting every other good into perspective. As the universal equivalent, money is the value that underlies that of every other commodity. What makes a commodity valuable is not just its particular qualities to be enjoyed but its capacity to be turned into the cash that can be used to procure further value anywhere, that can be deployed for the purchase of anything and everything one needs or desires. One pursues other goods therefore not simply for their own sake—one might not, in fact, find much enjoyment in them oneself—but because they can be converted into cash. Money gains in this way the ability to motivate all other motives since, whatever else one desires, one can also seek the possibility of making money thereby. By bringing them all under a single desire, money collects the diversity of all motives into one; it thereby absorbs particular desires within itself, submerging the limited value of all such objects of desire beneath the unspecifiable and potentially unlimited desirability of money itself.[33]

In similar fashion, however useful or valuable one's own pursuits might be for oneself or others, one's overriding purpose is to convert those pursuits to God, to make them all the occasion for God-directedness. Any and all such goods are so convertible; however diverse they may be, the desires for them are to be collected together under the overarching objective of gaining something that lies beyond them all and that thereby both gives them value and reveals their limited value in their own right. God is the universal equivalent of all objects of value in that their ultimate, underlying value is to enable Godwardness.

Although relativized, the other pursuits that fall under one's God project can of course remain valuable in and of themselves. Presumably one is pursuing them because one thinks they have a part to play in God's own mission of service to the world's good; they are part of one's effort to align one's own will with that of God. But that value to oneself and others is not in itself a stopping point, a self-contained value apart from such efforts to align oneself with God, in the way that being wholly and entirely invested in their attainment per se would seem to require.

Because no one pursuit has a monopoly on it, being God directed is not directly bought by, never simply dependent on, the successful achievement of any particular, mundane pursuit (even were it to be part of the effort to further the kingdom of God in this world). One can orient oneself to God whatever the tasks one assumes and therefore whatever one's success or failure in undertaking them. This is not simply because, as is the case with money, if one fails in one venture, there is always another one to take its place, another way to turn a profit. (The poor remain hungry but one can find some other way to align one's will with God's in the attempt to further God's kingdom.) Indeed—and here is a strong dissimilarity with the relationship of money to commodity pursuit—one's God project can be furthered despite the failure of each and every mundane one; there is simply no direct relationship between the successful pursuit of mundane projects and successful pursuit of devotion to God as one's life project. One cannot make money without some success in attaining goods convertible into cash because the one directly feeds the other. Godwardness can be achieved, to the contrary, despite the failure on its own terms of every other project designed to serve it.

This is in part because God will make up the difference; one is unsuccessful in eliminating poverty but one can leave it to God to nonetheless bring in the kingdom. But it is also because these very failures themselves can be God directed. One fails to eradicate poverty but such failure is turned to God through lament, repentance, and hope for greater success in renewed efforts to do God's will.

This dissimilarity with money is a function of a more general one. Unlike the relationship between the pursuit of other commodities and the pursuit of money, here mundane projects do not build up; they do not add up in any cumulative way, like a capital asset, so as to incrementally further one's life project of orienting oneself to God. Those other projects do not, in other words, take the form of bankable assets that one can draw on later for purposes of furthering one's God orientation. Not even the successful use of such mundane projects for purposes of God orientation provides such a bankable asset. The fact that one repented and sought forgiveness yesterday is of no account if one does not do the same thing today. That one praised God when things were going well is no basis for expecting one to exhibit an equally focused God orientation in times of trouble. Previous successes in orienting oneself to God cannot be stored up like money and easily converted into new orientations in changed circumstances. In some significant sense, therefore, one is always starting over at each moment, assuming the task of conversion afresh, however steady one's devotion to God has been up until that point. Because one remains a sinner, saved despite oneself in Christ, repeated lapses in God-directedness are to be expected; progress in a religious life project rarely displays a constancy in which present successes build seamlessly on past ones.

This need not, however, be a focus for worry. Because progress is assured through the grace of Christ within one, one can cast one's cares on God, who is ultimately responsible for carrying them to successful completion. One has the grace of Christ in ways that continuing sin does not threaten: one is saved *as* the sinner one remains by virtue of Christ's grace within one. Christ and his Spirit provide the ever-available motor for making over oneself, from sinner to saint, even though that transition is never complete in this life.

Apart from Christ, then, conversion represents no simple transition between old and new in oneself; one has not been wiped completely clean of sin and set on a new path of righteousness, to be jealously guarded and policed going forward in an effort to avoid the least fault, through the powers of one's newfound purity. Yet the transition from life without Christ to life with him is, indeed, a fundamentally absolute change of that kind, a qualitative change not properly subject to degrees. Because it represents an absolute change (from life without Christ to life with him), yet one not threatened by the ups and downs of one's own religious life (as some purported change from sinner to saint would be), conversion does not set into motion a juridical form of self-examination concerned about the least lapse in what one expects to be a seamless process of growth toward saintliness. One does not expect one's conversion to mean one has passed from sinner to saint, a transition thereby threatened by any post-conversion fault. While one has an interest no doubt in making progress in saintliness, gone is any anxiety-fed need for constant self-monitoring in the way finance-dominated capitalism would like, to assure that one is indeed making every effort in striving toward complete God-wardness. One confesses one's faults neither to exhibit a soul denying submission before one's superior nor primarily to keep a record of lapses in progress toward conformity with God's will, but as an expression of humility before the God upon whose grace one depends for any and all progress one makes oneself. Rather than being tallied against one's account, one can be assured one's sins are forgiven, their burden erased, when casting them upon Christ's mercy in confession. One can honestly admit faults without fear, assured of God's mercy in Christ. It is not the lapse that threatens to separate one from Christ but the refusal to confess it, out of fear and a lack of trust in God's graciousness.

Without the anxiety that comes from overinvestment in mundane tasks, one is able to act with a certain detachment toward them, knowing that one is not what one is in fact doing: one can in this way act, for example, as an employee as if one were not. This certainly means the tasks one undertakes at work cannot be taken to exhaust one's identity—and should not be pursued in any all-consuming fashion that would suggest as much. It means one is not bound to them in the identity one assumes in working on oneself in pursuit of God. If one were no longer to be doing this, one's orientation to God would not need to be harmed. It is also to remind oneself of the fact that Christian commitments trump others. The fact that one's Christian commitments are to be relevant in every circumstance means one must constantly question whether, and if so exactly how, what one is asked to do is genuinely compatible with those Christian commitments. They might not in fact be so compatible. In every case, other commitments should be held lightly in case either one's fortunes or one's Christian commitments take one out of them.

Every such commitment will indeed be lost to one at death, and, if restored at the end of time, every such commitment will take a new form beyond one's imagining. Do not then disinvest in what one is doing now by imagining doing something else equally mundane but by doing the same thing now in light of what it will one day become through Christ. Do it with the intention of transforming it, in ways never fully successful in this life, in light of what the world will become when God will be all in all and Christ fully manifest.

Working as though not working does not necessarily mean one suspects such tasks are not worth doing now, with an eye to ones that might bring greater present satisfaction (although it might). One may well find satisfaction in such pursuits (which provide reasons for thanks and praise of God). But the point in that case is not to find satisfaction solely in them but to glorify God in thanks and praise by way of them. One is to that extent distanced from such satisfactions, indifferent to their genuine charms, in that, whatever their degree, one is oriented by way of them to what lies beyond them.

Oriented beyond all mundane pursuits and the satisfactions they bring in and of themselves, this is a peculiar self-project in that the self is neither its ultimate object nor the ultimate motor for its attainment. One participates in a project in which God brings one to God. Michel Foucault is therefore wrong, I think, to assume that all such projects of self-fashioning by definition, and therefore in the Christian case as well, make the self the primary object of the practice. According to him, one is for example either to evacuate oneself (in Christianity) or prove the master of oneself (in Stoicism).

Lots of projects of self-fashioning—Platonic, Stoic-influenced—promise to distance one from oneself, from the ordinary subject of conventional roles and tasks, but they tend to do so by getting one to see oneself from the wider perspective of the whole.[34] They want one to turn from one's own limited reason, the partial perspective of self-interest that would make external harms to oneself something to be lamented, to the reason of the universe that directs the whole and everything in it for the good. Such forms of self-transcendence merely bring one into resigned, undisturbed alignment with what Christianity views as a finite and fallen world. Instead, from a Christian viewpoint, God, who is not the world, is what one should be made over into, one's own desires brought into perfect alignment with God's will for that world, now fallen into sin and needing a renewal as deep as its original creation, a kind of recreation. The sin that runs rampant in one's self and in the world as one knows it is what stands in the way of all that. Conformity to God thereby interrupts all desires for conformity with the cosmos, which in one's own day amounts to the wider world of the market.[35] "Plunging oneself into the totality of the world," as Seneca advised, is just what one is *not* to do.[36]

What I have shown, then, is the way Christianity can re-envision, and thereby contest, the sort of subject that finance-dominated capitalism encourages for its own purposes of profit maximization. The point where finance-dominated capitalism inserts itself into people's lives is also its place of vulnerability. As Foucault might say (were he to have addressed this particular trajectory of neoliberalism since his death), finance-dominated capitalism tries to conduct, in quite thorough-going ways, the conduct of others, conduct that takes the form of other people's projects of self-formation, in an all-out effort to get the most out of them. But in that very process it leaves itself open to challenge. Such forms of self-fashioning are always at least potentially open for redirection in ways that finance-dominated capitalism cannot countenance. Resistance of that sort—by way of the very demand for self-formation that finance-dominated capitalism enforces—becomes in this way specific to the particular way one is being controlled; it turns the very thing that is intended to further finance-dominated interests against that system.[37]

Foucault himself seemed to suggest at times that such a disruptive counter-conduct could be produced simply by ridding what neoliberalism requires of its character as a demand. One could remain such a subject—a self-productive kind of enterprise self—but without being subjected, that is, by refusing any imperative of obedience or conformity to general law in the process (which would help explain his interest in ancient Stoicism—self-mastery replaces obedience and individuality confounds requirements of simple uniformity in conformity).[38] What I have shown instead is the way a counter-conduct can be produced in the point-by-point disruption of the specific mechanisms for conducting conduct found in finance-dominated capitalism.

The Christian character of that counter-conduct is significant. Foucault recognized that the sort of Christian subject formation that fed into contemporary ways of controlling conduct—self-surveillance for the sake of total obedience to religious superiors, juridically informed projects of self-improvement based on postbaptismal expectations of perfection, and so on—did not exhaust Christianity; that remainder resurfaced with a vengeance, particularly at the time of the Reformation, to contest Christian ways of conducting the conduct of others by such means.[39] What I have shown is the continued relevance of such Christian forms of counter-conduct for contesting not just Christian forms of conducting the conduct of others but the finance-dominated capitalism that transmutes and extends such techniques into the present.

4

Nothing but the Present

Maximum profitability requires not simply perfect compliance with company demands but complete attention to task. Whatever one might be asked to do, concentrated focus on the matter at hand is required for maximally efficient performance—blocking everything else from one's mind in order to get the job done as expeditiously as possible.

The mechanisms for assuring perfect compliance suggest as much—that maximum attentiveness to task is also required. Total commitment to one's work means total investment at every moment, complete absorption in the task at hand, absent all diversions or distractions of time and energy elsewhere. If one's only desire is to do what others ask, the whole of one's attention is naturally captured completely by the task in front of one; work arrangements, like tight flow, which demand total attention to task at every moment, are indeed one way of promoting just such an evacuation of one's own will and its replacement by the will of another.

Along with others like it in finance-dominated capitalism, this way of relating to present circumstances—in a totally absorbed and focused fashion—keeps one from stepping back from what one is currently doing and reassessing the situation, from deciding that one would rather do otherwise, from making decisions that might redirect one's energies, pull one in new directions. This way of relating to the present keeps one, in short, from imagining doing anything differently.

Scarcity and Present Preoccupation, and Their Temporal Effects in Finance-Dominated Capitalism

The scarcity of time and resources enforced by profit-maximizing firms makes the present task urgent for workers and therefore preoccupying and all-consuming. There is no time to waste because a pressing deadline is looming. One does not have the luxury of waiting to see what might happen; no time exists for extended reflection nor can one defer decisions until tomorrow.

Should one damage materials along the way, no further supplies are waiting in the wings. No slack exists in the production process—no spare time, no spare parts, no reserves of any sort—to be forgiving of the least fault. Everything has to be done right the first time. Indeed, one likely has neither sufficient time nor resources to even finish the task unless one gives it one's full, immediate attention.

Finance-dominated management practices in this way take advantage of, and push to an extreme, the mind-focusing, efficiency-maximizing effects of scarcity common in everyday life.[1] Having one dart with a single second to hit the dartboard (rather than ten darts with a leisurely ten minutes to play) encourages one to pay very close attention to each throw. It concentrates the mind on the task at hand and prompts careful consideration of all that can be done to succeed within that short timeframe with such limited resources.

Indeed, totally preoccupied with present performance, one engages in the very sort of tight time and resource management that made the task urgent to begin with; one makes maximally efficient use of time and resources so as to help rid the production process of any slack. One puts every moment and material to good use, without the slightest waste, with nothing left over.

Efficiency effects are produced here by having to start, so to speak, with only a very small suitcase.[2] A very small suitcase requires one, instead of just throwing things in haphazardly while talking on the phone with friends about one's upcoming trip, to give full attention to the packing. That means packing very carefully, by trying to fit in the most one can, leaving no space unused, rolling every item up as tightly as possible, weighing up all the tradeoffs—what one is forced to leave behind—of every decision to include something, and so on. Those with big suitcases—plenty of time and resources—have no such impetus to pack efficiently. Lots of time and resources make one inattentive to task, thereby wasting both time and space. One procrastinates, putting off the task to a more opportune time that never comes. One does not pack everything one needs because one fails to make the most of the space, or one miscalculates and weighs oneself down with items that turn out to be unnecessary.

Everyone with limited time and resources in finance-dominated capitalism does the same, is subject to the same scarcity-propelled efficiency dynamics. So, for example, unemployed or underemployed and therefore short on cash and without reserves of any kind, one becomes completely absorbed in the effort to make the rent that is due tomorrow, stretching one's cash as far as it will go, purchasing everything else one needs at the least possible expense, carefully weighing up the costs of even the most minor purchases. And in each case, too, what especially focuses the mind is the likely consequence of failing in the effort to be so efficient and missing the mark: being fired or demoted, in the previous workplace example, or being evicted, in the case here. The situation in the present that calls for action is not simply urgent, requiring immediate attention, then, but something on the order of an emergency. Everything needs to be thrown at it since the ramifications of failure are so dire. Something has to be done right away to make the rent or the consequences will be disastrous.

This sort of preoccupation with an urgent present task has further temporal effects. First, the present upon which one is focusing becomes depleted of its usual temporal dimensions. The present becomes so absorbing that it pushes consideration of past and future out of present consciousness. One no longer thinks of past and future in the present; they for all intents and purposes disappear. Preoccupation with the present emergency shrinks down past and future dimensions of the present, leaving nothing but the present, a bare present, to which one's consciousness is captive. One simply does not have the time or energy, for example, to think about tomorrow—say, the future consequences of actions taken now to address the immediate problem, or the likely next task needing to be addressed at work. Doing any of that would simply prove an unwanted distraction from what one needs to be totally focused on doing now. One does not in fact have any unused cognitive capacity to give to such thoughts about the future; one's cognitive bandwidth is completely absorbed in the present task, with no unused capacities left over for deployment elsewhere.[3]

For similar reasons, present preoccupations incapacitate prospective memory: one can recall as easily as ever what one had for lunch yesterday but what one intended yesterday to do today slips from one's mind. One tends to forget past resolutions about the future in which one is now living, especially when such resolutions might prove distracting from the present urgent task. One forgets to take one's medication, for example, while preoccupied with making the rent.[4]

Because the future is not considered in the present— because it is being actively pushed from one's mind—the future consequences of present action tend to be discounted much more heavily than would ordinarily be the case. This is the second major temporal effect of scarcity-induced preoccupation with the present. The future is always discounted to some extent, because it is not a sure thing and because it tends to be less salient, harder to imagine, than the present. But such a tendency is now severely aggravated. The costs in future of actions taken now fail to be weighed up with any degree of appropriateness; they tend to be overwhelmed by any immediate present benefits of action taken now to attend to urgent tasks.[5]

One is therefore almost irresistibly inclined to borrow against the future, even at severe cost. One is inclined to use for present gain what could otherwise be put to good use later on, leaving that much less for subsequent purposes. One uses up the time and resources that could be put to use later on, so that one has even less time and fewer resources when new urgent tasks roll around. Thus, using every moment now, one finds oneself behind at the start of any new project. By taking an advance on future wages to pay the rent this month, one has even less next month to pay it. Even if additional costs are accrued—for example, very high interest payments on payday loans—the seriousness of those costs are dismissed in the present. One simply has to have the money now and will deal with the consequences later; they are not a present concern. Even if

complete exhaustion is the likely price to be paid later for putting every waking moment to good use now while on the job,
one assumes that risk without giving it a second's thought.[6]

In this way, people pushed by scarcity into highly efficient,
rational-choice maximization in the present tend to be anything
but rational when it comes to calculations with a bearing on
the future. They are prone to very accurate cost-benefit analy-
ses in the present.[7] Short on cash, people in poverty will, for
example, choose to save fifty dollars whether it seems a lot or
a little relative to the cost of the particular item to be purchased:
fifty dollars is always fifty dollars—just that much less to pay
one's rent with. But the same people will not hesitate to take
out a loan at 500 percent interest if that is the only available
means to pay the rent due tomorrow.

In this way, the scarcity that promotes preoccupation with
the present is exacerbated in the future. One is even less prepared
to cope with future eventualities than one was to address present ones. Future eventualities become for that reason all the
more preoccupying, forcing one into even more efficient use
of ever more meager resources, with the same stultifying effects
on future planning, so as to produce a kind of self-feeding
spiral. The future always comes as a shock, not simply because
one has not had the time before to think about what was likely
to happen but because actions taken to address present tasks
had a severe impact on resources necessary to cope with later
ones.[8]

Insofar as the present is shorn of its temporal dimensions,
past and future evacuated from present consciousness, successive events become a disconnected sequence of presents.[9] This
is the third main temporal consequence of present preoccupation. What happened before is no longer held in present remembrance, nor is the future a matter of present anticipation.

Rather than being collected together in present awareness, past and future are only registered as presents in their moment of happening and are gone as soon as they appear. Rather than being retained in the forms of memory and expectation in the present, they come into and out of consciousness as a discontinuous series of pure presents. Present consciousness becomes itself in this way a dispersed rather than collected consciousness; one is never presently aware of time building up, and therefore it becomes very difficult to construct a coherent narrative of what has been happening to one over the course of time. One's life is just one thing after another, a sequence of fires coming out of nowhere that one is repeatedly forced to try to put out.

The same sort of time-effects that are produced by efficiency-promoting measures of finance-dominated capitalism also come about by way of attempts within finance-dominated capitalism to generate profits through market mirroring. One must react immediately to the signals sent by the market— putting in the appropriate order to buy or sell a stock, changing one's employees' time schedules accordingly, and so on—and that means pushing out of one's mind thoughts of past and future. The intensity of the present moment in all its urgency is all that matters. Thinking of past and future would at best foment a lag in responsiveness to the market; at worst it could hinder appropriate reactions to the signals that the market is presently sending. As a stock trader, for example, memory of past failures can make me lose my nerve and question what my gut is telling me now. Remembering past triumphs can tempt me to be overly confident about decisions I have already made and lead me to ignore contrary market signals in the present.[10]

Particularly on a random-walk, regression-to-mean view of them, financial markets have no memory. According to such a view, past performance is no indicator of future performance.

Like the throw of a dice, the die-face that comes up on one throw tells one nothing about the next; therefore do not let the memory of one hundred sixes in a row prove a distraction. A market in which the present has no relation of dependence on the past, and in which the future that will one day become the present has no relations of dependence on the present, is to be mirrored by persons who practice a similar sort of temporal dissociation. "Traders [for example] work to isolate one decision from the next, dividing now from then. In the trade, there is no past and no projection ahead. The present moment takes precedence. . . . Traders [therefore] work hard to maintain the kind of division that breaks down any narrative that might arise from a series of successive losses and gains. It takes active efforts to break down the sense of continuity that comes with repeated success or failure."[11] One must "segment time into small, disconnected increments to stop . . . narratives from building" and "treat each trade as if it had no effect on the next."[12]

"Where a primacy of the present . . . [so] ruthlessly disintegrates the narrative fabric that attempts to reform around it," it becomes very hard to see how one could "even [picture] coherently, let alone [devise] strategies to produce, some radically different future."[13] "The breakdown of temporality suddenly releases this present of time from all the activities and intentionalities that might focus it and make it the space of praxis."[14] Captivated by the bare present, one is hindered from "[pursuing] projects [that extend] over time, or [thinking] cogently about the production of a future significantly better than time present and time past."[15]

Similar consequences accrue from simply shortening the temporal horizons of past and future in present decision-making. When one does consider the past and future in the present, one never thinks very far back or forward into either.

This is the fourth major temporal consequence of present pre-occupation: only the immediate past or future has any relevance; anything beyond that drops away.

A number of features of finance-dominated capitalism encourage the production of such a present that lacks temporal depth. Analogous to a lack of photographic depth (which concerns the degree to which what's in front of or behind the main object of attention is in focus too), one loses the capacity to focus on anything at any temporal remove from the present, which constitutes the primary object of attention. Anything too far off in time—whether in the past or the future—loses its salience; it drops off one's radar screen. The past and future horizons of present decision-making in this way become extremely short.[16]

Encouraging this development in finance-dominated capitalism is what sociologists call environmental dynamism.[17] Market conditions are changing so rapidly that one is discouraged from thinking very far ahead or back. There is no point in thinking far ahead since it is hard to predict what circumstances will be like then. And there is little point in thinking far back since so much has happened between then and now to make that past irrelevant to present circumstances.

Instead one hovers right at the edge of the about-to-be-past and the about-to-be-present future, watching the present right at the cusp of its moving away into the past and its coming into existence from the future. One must catch the present right before it becomes the past, selling a stock, for example, just before everyone else does in ways that bring about the present value's demise. And then move on. And one behaves similarly with respect to a future about to arrive: "Because it is always moving forward in time, [the market] always remains uncertain. [The trader's] work [therefore] exists in a just

emerging future, one step ahead of the market."[18] One anticipates in increments of a second what is to come.

Market instability and volatility in this way exaggerate the
importance of temporal strategies commonly used to cope with
the uncertain future that is everyone's lot in life. "Life ebbs as I
speak: so seize each day, and grant the next no credit," as Horace famously puts it.[19] Take what one can get now, because it is
unclear what tomorrow might bring. The pleasures of the past
are gone; future ones are uncertain; the present is, in any case,
the only time in which such pleasure is actually experienced.
Enjoy what one can now, therefore, without bothering to give
much thought to what happened in the past or what might
come in the future. The only pasts or futures to be considered
are ones with an immediate, unavoidable bearing on one's present happiness. With the instability of the future a much more
salient matter than perhaps in any previous time in modern
history—at any moment one might lose one's job or one's shirt
in the market—such an Epicurean foreshortened view of the
present might seem quite in order. As a former investment
banker interviewed by the ethnographer Karen Ho put such
sentiments: "It is all about today, and . . . whether one can make
money today, and if you can't make money today, you are out
of there. . . . You need to be thinking I'm going to get as much
as I can today because you don't know what is going to happen
tomorrow."[20] Or, a fundamentally Stoic approach to the present
proves attractive in the interest of gaining greater control over
one's life in a disturbingly turbulent economic environment.
One has the power at present to turn a profit; take those profits
now, before changed circumstances steal the opportunity of
doing so away. One cannot undo past mistakes and who knows
what the future might hold, thus concentrate on reacting appropriately to the opportunities presented by the market right

now. That present reaction is the only thing one can be certain to control. Join both Stoics and Epicureans in "liberating oneself not only from worries about the future, but also from the burden of the past, in order to concentrate on the present moment; in order either to enjoy it, or act within it."[21]

Extremely short time horizons in decision-making are also simply a function of the way profits are generated in finance-dominated capitalism. Profits are typically made in the short rather than long term. Investments that will prove profitable only over the long haul—say, investing in heavy equipment where the profits from doing so are to be cashed out slowly the more one sells—are typically avoided in favor of ones with the capacity to turn a profit very quickly—say, taking over a company with the intention of selling it as soon as its stock market value goes up. Even in long-term ventures, decision-making favors immediate results. Since the value of a company is constantly reassessed on a stock market, management decisions favor actions with an immediate impact on stock value—such as, layoffs—rather than ones—like a new marketing strategy—whose success will only become apparent far in the future. When companies are managed simply to promote shareholder value, absolutely no premium is put on long-term planning; planning to assure ongoing company profitability over an extended period of time becomes almost passé.[22]

Long-term investments are to be avoided because of the market volatility typical of finance-dominated capitalism: the market can move out from you in ways that make investment decisions in the past no longer advisable. Short-term investments are, in other words, a way of avoiding the future risks incurred by investment decisions now. One can move on, cash out, and try one's hand at something else that will have become the more profitable option later on. In rapidly changing conditions, long-term investments simply amplify exposure to risk and limit the ability to move quickly to take advantage of newly unfolding opportunities. Contracts regarding financial assets typically for these reasons have very short expiration dates; one has the option of buying a currency, say, at a fixed price not ten years from now but next week or a day from now. One does not want to be tied down by any investment decision for very long. Ideally, indeed, deals should be completed almost immediately. The shorter the time between purchase and sale the better. Therefore, something like simple arbitrage becomes the gold standard: one buys on one market and sells simultaneously on another in order to pocket the difference between the prices of the same financial assets across them. Japanese yen are cheaper to buy with U.S. dollars in one market rather than another; buy them, then, in the one and sell them at once on the other.[23]

Short-term, finance-dominated investment decisions in this way run directly contrary to the usual company tactics for dealing with volatility. In producing anything for sale, one is likely to face unexpected downturns in demand or interruptions in transport, for example because bad weather kept shoppers from stores or trucks off the road. Long-terms commitments become a way of smoothing over exposure to the risks produced by such volatility in the business environment. If one has a good product that customers want, ups and downs like this will even out over the long haul if one simply stays the course. Where volatility is no longer an external impediment to turning a profit but internal to the business model, as in finance-dominated capitalism, staying the course makes little sense. Profits are now directly geared to that volatility; volatility is the means to them. Only if stock values go up and down, rapidly and steeply, can one hope to make an enormous amount of money from the stock market impact of management decisions. One turns such a profit only by reacting the right way to the changing signals the market is giving. If one stays the course and fails to move in line with market volatility—say, by refusing to close stores or lay off workers after a bad winter cuts sales and plays havoc with inventory—the value of company stock might plummet.

Profits, in short, are typically made in finance-dominated capitalism by directly playing on market volatility rather than by simply attempting to avoid its impact. Short-termism becomes not merely a way of avoiding future risk but a primary means of profiting from the very volatility that produces risk. Prices go up and down, and one tries to capitalize on that very fact. Doing so, however, requires speed. Profiting from something in rapid movement requires equally rapid movement from you. As soon as the opportunity appears, pounce on it; there is no profit in waiting. The longer one holds one's position the more likely it is that the opportunity for profit will be gone, seized by others and no longer available. If a stock is overpriced, sell it as quickly as possible before everyone else does and the price comes down. Decision-making that considers the long term is beside the point when profit becomes a function of speed, a matter of quick reaction time.

Profit within capitalism is always a function of the turnover time on investment: the more rapid that turnover the better.[24] Better to sell every widget that the equipment has the capacity of making as quickly as possible, rather than in drips and drabs over an extended time frame. But finance-dominated capitalism, because it is not dependent on slow processes of making and selling actual things, allows such turnover time to be nearly instantaneous. Ordinarily, one has to wait to produce things and then wait for them to be sold. But a derivative contract, for example, creates its product as soon as it is drawn up—its product is the linkage it creates between financial assets themselves. One enjoys right now, for instance, the assurance of being in the money if the value of the asset one holds drops below a certain point relative to some other. And such contracts can be settled just as quickly, because nothing but money changes hands. If one bets the price of hogs will go up next week, the bet is not settled through any actual exchange of hogs with another party—which would take some time—but by a simple cash transfer from loser to winner. And every such contract can itself be sold at once; one does not have to wait to see what the price of hogs will be next week but can turn a profit right now by selling the contract itself to someone else. Profit-making by way of arbitrage—simultaneous buying in one market and selling in another—becomes again in this way the extreme that proves finance-dominated capitalism's penchant for the short term.

The simultaneity that characterizes buying and selling in arbitrage is typical of other forms of transactions in finance-dominated capitalism and helps contribute to the deflation of past and future in present awareness. For example, it is common in financial transactions to take simultaneous long and short positions to avoid facing the unhedged consequences of either. A bet that a stock will decline is often simultaneously offset by a bet that it will rise, in order to stem potential losses. Moreover, efficiency measures to increase profitability often involve the network coordination of actors in teams. By way of computerized groupware, every team member interacts with every other in real time rather than in the sort of linear series established via a production line.[25] In all such simultaneous processing, actions and reactions follow one another so quickly, in nearly real time, that they lose any easy sequencing with reference to past and future. What I am responding to comes at me so quickly that it loses its past character, and my reactions to it are so immediate as no longer to seem the future of any preceding prompt. Even spatially quite distant events appear concurrently with my present consciousness; no time lag is required to bring their occurrence to my attention. Instead, every event seems to be interacting with every other in real time to produces effects, and it therefore becomes very difficult to make sense of such effects by telling a story in which events unroll, one from another, over time.[26] Unable to place myself along a timeline, it becomes difficult to see myself as part of any ongoing historical trajectory, moving from the past into the future, that I might intervene within and interrupt.[27]

Instantaneous transaction times do not just have the effect of making anything very far in the past or future irrelevant to present decision-making; they also shrink the economically relevant present down to almost nothing. And this is a fifth major temporal effect of finance-disciplined preoccupations with the present. The time in which profits are taken is so accelerated that it drops below the duration required for present awareness of it, below even the shortest "attention-span of lived consciousness."[28] Transactions are processed via computer in nanoseconds, too quickly to be experienced.[29] Not simply depleted of any memory of the past or anticipation of the future, the present moment for profit-taking comes itself in this way to have no duration; it extends no farther than the instant. If one intends to turn a profit in financial dealings, one should not try to draw out the present beyond the moment—say, by wishing or hoping that what is happening now might last. It will not, and thinking that it might simply hinders one's quick reaction to new opportunities for profit down the road. One should not tarry in the present, so as to keep it from sliding into a past that one can forget about; every extra moment one dwells on it is one more opportunity lost. "Wishing, hoping, praying ... these expressions of individual desire extend the present moment forward in time" in ways that "alter the time frame of a trader's decision-making capacities" for the worse. "They undermine the trader's ability to react" in the ways a changing market calls for—on a moment-by-moment basis.[30]

One might think that such short-term profiteering would come back to bite one down the road, in much the way short-termism on the part of time- and resource-strapped workers and debtors does. They suffer later from actions taken in the present to put out fires; those actions make them less well pre-pared and even more time- and resource-strapped when trying to cope with future eventualities. In similar fashion, eschewing long-term investments in favor of management tactics with immediate effects on company stock valuations will eventually, one would think, hurt company profits and send the company's stock tumbling. As one scholar notes, "No long-term strategy is ... potentially self-defeating in that [companies] often find themselves making drastic changes only to realize months or weeks later that those changes were unnecessary, premature, and extremely costly."[31] It hardly seems cost-effective over the long term to be shutting down offices and firing workers one day to keep profits up during a market downturn, only to set offices up and begin hiring again under changed market condi-tions the next. With a "strategy of no strategy," companies seem "unable to peer into the future and realize that they will prob-ably have to rehire soon after they have just fired."[32] In a similar fashion, quick fixes to machines to avoid any interruptions in tight flow tend to be poor fixes that time eventually uncovers, requiring much more time and energy to correct at a later date than they would have if fixed properly the first time.[33]

Short-term trading might have the effect (as we see in the next chapter) of so magnifying volatility that enormous market downturns at some point become all but unavoidable.

But typically those paying the long-term costs of short-sightedness are not the same ones reaping the short-term profits.[34] Indeed, that is one of the points of profit-taking in the short term; by the time the costs of that sort of profit-taking become apparent, one is gone. The ones who have to pay are the ones who fail to move as fast.

Thus, the CEO paid in stock options can cash out and move onto a new job before the short-term tactics to raise stock values take any obvious toll on a company's profit margins. It is the later holders of stock who suffer, along with company workers, paid in wages rather than stock options, whose livelihood depends on longer-term employment (at a company that therefore has to remain in business over the long haul). When the lack of investment in new equipment takes its toll and the company tanks, they are the ones whose livelihood is compromised.

Indeed, their paying the long-term costs of a lack of planning typically directly feeds short-term profit-taking by financial means. Layoffs and plant closings, one might surmise, are often the consequence of poor planning: the future turns out to be different from the expectations about it as reflected, for example, in past hiring decisions. But those layoffs and plant closings at worker expense only make the company's stock rise, because of the way they cut costs and increase company profits immediately.

Short-term profit takers are always standing at the ready to take advantage of the failures of others to do long-range planning. Who benefits, for instance, when workers are forced into greater time efficiencies by prior actions that cut into time available for later projects? The company concerned with maximum utilization of resources at every moment. Who benefits from the high-interest loans that people without money are desperate to take out to make ends meet? Or from the greater efficiencies in meager resource management that poor people are forced into to service their debt? The payday loan provider or the secondhand car loan originator, who can make money not simply on exorbitant interest payments but by immediately selling the loans themselves so that they might be repackaged into high-yield bonds for quick sale to others. The unfortunate consequences for oneself of bad future planning become in these ways the direct means of profit for someone else with no particular interest in long-term investments or concern about the future consequences of their own short-term profit-taking.

In general, people without money become vulnerable to the future costs incurred by the shortsighted business decisions of people with money. People cannot move with the speed of money. People without the money to compensate for their slowness are therefore always liable to get burned by those with the money to increase their speed.

Money can be cashed out of investment in one company's stock and instantly repurposed, to purchase another company's stock. The movements of people, when following the ups and downs of such stock movements—fired from one company, looking for work at another—are much stickier, more costly for them, and therefore slower. Movements of people are not frictionless, like the movement of money, and bring with them substantial transaction costs, such as the need for retraining. Companies can close down underperforming operations and outsource them quite quickly to companies in areas of the world with lower labor costs; people cannot move as easily or as quickly to where the jobs are. Without the same liquidity, the ability to move as quickly in and out of investments—in a place, a job, a form of training—people without money become vulnerable to people enjoying the speed of movement, the liquidity, that comes from having money (or other capital assets).

Across the board, exploitation in finance-dominated capitalism comes about by taking advantage of relative differences in speed. It is because the great majority of investors in the stock market do not have the benefit of sophisticated real-time data analysis (or do not have the time to bother with it) that they can be taken advantage of by people who do; the slowness of the former group in reacting to news means greater profits for those who engage in instantaneous, moment-by-moment trading. It is the fact that companies can move their operations in the way their employees cannot that enables them to pay those workers less; the latter are held hostage to the former's mobility. Employees in effect pay with reduced wages and benefits for the decisions of such companies to remain immobile. States do the same, lowering corporate tax rates, for example, with a huge impact on state coffers, in order to keep companies from picking up their operations and leaving.[35]

The degree and liquidity of one's resources have in fact a major impact on whether focus on the present has the capacity to affect one's future adversely. So, for example, the person whose bad long-range planning squeezes them for time on future projects but leaves them with cash to spare is significantly better off than the person squeezed for both time and money—not simply because they retain more assets but because the one they retain, money, is the more liquid one. If one is exhausted from spending all of one's time on an urgent deadline, one can pay someone to do the life-maintenance chores one no longer has the time or energy for when the next project rolls

around, and in that way relieve the burden. Out of cash and
further in debt, the consequences of one's shortsightedness are,
to the contrary, largely irremediable.[36]

Short-termism does not in itself, simply by making the
future less salient, bring about bad consequences for those with
large reserves of liquid assets. This is in great part because their
reasons for being preoccupied with the present are different
from those of time- and resource-strapped workers or the poor
without cash savings. For those with spare cash to invest, the
present has urgency not because it is a fire—an emergency to
cope with—but because it is an opportunity for profit that
simply needs to be seized quickly before it is gone. One typically does not invest every penny in ways that would make one
cash-poor in the future. One retains plenty of money for future
use, so as to be poised to take advantage of the next moment's
possible profit-making opportunity. Borrowing does retain the
attractiveness typical of those who are present-preoccupied.
One is indeed likely to take out a loan to limit the amount of
one's own money tied up in such an investment and to increase
one's possible profits through leverage. But such loans are
clearly discretionary rather than forced by indigence. One often
therefore retains the funds to pay them off; they are taken out
simply for convenience—to enable freer movement in future
by leaving more of one's own money available—and for profit-
maximization purposes. One also retains the possibility of
getting one's money back (and repaying any loan) by dumping
the investment itself right away, by selling it to someone else.
If one does sustain a loss, so what? One has more than enough
money to weather it and make a possible killing the next time
opportunity calls.

In this way, those with large reserves of liquid assets tend
to move in relatively carefree fashion from one present to the

next without suffering any harm. The present recedes into the past without any bearing on the next present, which arrives free and clear, without the burden of anything that preceded it. Presents succeed each other in a disconnected fashion that is breezy and untroubled for all that; the series of disconnected presents produced by the short-term investments of those with money to burn is far from disconcerting or disturbing, nothing like the series of unexpected storms that arrive one by one out of the blue because one's efforts to cope with earlier troubles left one completely unprepared for the next. People without liquidity "actually need to plan in order to survive."[37]

Especially for those without resources or liquid capital, the constantly changing character of the present assumes the tenor of a paralyzing instability. One is not secure enough in the present to make it the basis for decision-making with a bearing on one's future, and the present is nothing one can count on to provide a reliable basis for decision-making that would take the future into account. How do I know that my judgments now about how best to improve my lot in life will not be disconfirmed tomorrow? What confidence do I have that a decision to seek further training over the next few years will pay off? Like a corporation sitting on its cash in times of crisis, people who are buffeted by any shock because of a lack of liquid reserves easily become paralyzed by indecision, unwilling to invest or take any action that might put them at risk later on. They become anything but risk-taking, resource-daring, opportunity-seizing entrepreneurs.[38]

Vulnerable to the downside risks of a constantly changing present, the present awareness of the resource-strapped person becomes fear infused: one feels under constant threat. One is unsure about one's ability to meet present challenges; fear of failure is always salient. And one realizes that what one has presently achieved can be lost at any moment. One is always aware, at every moment, of the insecure hold one has on anything currently enjoyed. One relates to the present with a constant sense of how precarious it is. There is nothing secure about one's present job, one's present pay; everything is always in danger, moment by moment, of slipping away.

Even if a myopic focus on the present allowed for imagining a different future, this fear-infused relationship to the present might make one reluctant to act to bring that future about. Imagining a different future is one thing; the temporal effects of present-preoccupation stop that. Wanting and willing a different future is another matter, dependent in great part on one's affective relationship to the present. Feeling fearful, being anxious rather than hopeful about possibilities afforded by the present, does away with that.[39]

People generally tend to be loss-averse, that is, they are more inclined to keep what they have than put it at risk for gain even when taking such a risk is a good bet. But the salience of downside risks for workers at every moment in finance-dominated capitalism—the awareness that one's job might be cut, pay docked, benefits slashed, or hours reduced, at any time, with the slightest provocation—exaggerates such loss aversion. It is not so much the having that makes one more loss-averse here. The more one has the more one has to lose and therefore the less likely one is to put it at risk for the sake of gain. I am much more likely to risk the loss of a dollar on a coin toss than I am to risk a million dollars, even if betting correctly on the toss would mean doubling my money. I have more than enough, thank you, and I will simply keep what I have. In the present case, instead, the evident dangers to anything presently enjoyed is what reinforces concern to avoid or stem losses whenever possible. One has nothing but the present to hang onto, which may well not amount to much—just some crummy, part-time job at low pay—but, given the obvious threat to it, one hangs onto it very tightly and refuses to let it go, even when letting go has the potential to bring a much brighter future. Fear might impel one to act—it is not necessarily paralyzing—but one is inclined to act simply in the interest of self-preservation. Fearful of loss in the present, one becomes satisfied with—or at least resigned to—the way things are and does what one can to keep things in place, by simply repelling any threat to the status quo as a form of self-defense.[40]

Christian Approaches to the Present

Christianity as I have been characterizing it also exhibits a preoccupation with the present; the present has an urgency that concentrates attention on it. By virtue of such an overlap in temporal sensibility, a Christian approach to the present has the capacity to infiltrate the way finance-dominated capitalism encourages one to relate to it, and in so doing disrupt it, since the reasons and effects of such a focus on the present moment are diametrically opposed in the two cases.

Christianity sees the urgency of the present in that each and every moment becomes the time for response to the constantly posed demand for conversion to God through Christ. "The 'remembrance of God' is a perpetual reference to God at every instant of life. Basil of Caesarea links it explicitly with the 'watch of the heart': 'We must keep watch over our heart, with all vigilance . . . to avoid ever losing the thought of God.'"[41] One has not a moment to lose when considering whether to devote one's life to God. One should not delay. The future will bring no improvement in circumstances; putting off the decision will bring one only closer to the death that will take away irrevocably the possibility of such a life-changing conversion. Wake up every day as if it were one's first and last, so that one gives the greatest attention to the time allotted and in that sense practice dying daily as Paul recommends.[42] Denied the ability to rest on one's laurels because of sin, one must continue to attend at every moment to the question of whether one has in fact turned one's life around, the degree to which one's current behavior would suggest as much. "Give heed to yourself, lest there be a hidden word in your heart" running against devotion to God.[43]

The present does not, however, become urgent here due to scarcity. One has everything one needs—more than one needs—to turn one's life around: the grace provided in Christ. In marked contrast to the efficiency-inducing scarcities of finance-dominated capitalism, it is the very fulsomeness of the provisions for conversion that makes the present an urgent matter, an opportunity to be seized with alacrity and put to good use. There is no point in looking longingly to any past or future with the capacity to make things easier: the time is ripe for action right now and never has been or will be any better. Delaying a present decision to turn one's life around, and neglecting to make the best of what is currently on offer out of a distracted sense of what was or might be, suggest one is simply never likely to turn one's life around, no matter how many times one is offered the opportunity to do so in the future. Any such distraction from the present moment is always available as an excuse in the future, so as to produce thereby a never-ending deferral of decision.

The present is urgent here not because the opportunities of the moment might be lost but because they are just so good, so perfectly suited to the predicament one is in and the needs one has, because of their not-to-be-passed-up character, so to speak. Instead of being here today and gone tomorrow, what allows one to turn one's life around in the present—the grace of Christ—is permanently on offer. It has no fleeting character. What prompts one to seize it right away is not the fear of missed opportunity, then, but the immediate, overwhelming attractiveness of the offer.

Nor is attention to the present moment sharpened here by an unforgiving environment in which one knows the least misstep could prove one's undoing. To the contrary, one attends to the task of the present—conversion to God—with the assurance of fault-forgiveness. No failings in the past or present can disrupt the efficacy of a grace designed specifically to save sinners. One has more than enough to get by, plenty of slack, in the form of grace, to make up for or cover over missteps in the effort to turn one's life around to God.

There is thus no point in harping on the past or worrying about the future—the present is one's only concern. Not because one cannot do anything about past mistakes or about an uncertain future—because neither is under one's control—but because one can let go of the past without consequence—one's sins are forgiven—and because the future will never be any more threatening than the present is. Contrary to the Stoic-inflected temporal sensibility of financial players, the present is no more under one's control than the past was or the future will be: at every moment in time, one is enabled to turn oneself to God only by God's grace and not by one's own power. The difficulties one may have in the future in trying to turn one's life around are therefore never greater than the ones one suffers now. The worries of today are more than sufficient as a matter for concern.

The fault-forgiveness surrounding the urgency of conversion in Christianity means that mistakes cannot be compounded here to produce the sort of scarcity trap typical of finance-disciplined preoccupations with the present. One is not able to make one's situation worse by time- and resource-depleting actions taken to cope with present circumstance. One's ongoing sinfulness does not have the power, like an unwisely assumed future debt obligation, to deplete the resources necessary to meet future demands. It is all right if the demands of the present keep one from planning for the future by storing up resources sufficient to meet unexpected eventualities to come. The fulsome character of grace means in any case that the need for such borrowing against the future disappears: one has all one needs now to meet the present challenge. And the resources necessary for conversion are simply not ones amenable to such efforts to storehouse them. Attempts to do so in fact mistake their nature, as they cannot be added to or subtracted from by one's own actions.

The odd way that fulsome resources for conversion are made repeatedly available, moment of decision after moment of decision, may be peculiar to grace in Christ, but it dovetails with practical suggestions for overcoming the strain on workers and the poor.[44] They need some slack, not simply to lessen unrelenting efficiency demands for time and resource management but to help them recover from mistakes that for them— and not for those with plenty of time and money—have devastating consequences, squeezing the very life out of them. They need a less volatile supply of resources so that they have what they need when they need it. As it stands, what one is paid— determined by base salary, the hours one works, and so on— goes up and down in ways that are completely unsynchronized with one's need to pay others. Workers are in fact making a loan to their employers by working for some time before they are paid—often at the end of the month. Why cannot employers make no-interest advances on worker paychecks in an equally routine fashion to help workers cover unexpected expenses or simply to help them out in case they come up short at the end of the month, rather than leaving them with high-interest payday loans as their only option? A world of measures might be taken to make life less difficult for those dogged by all-consuming emergencies, day after day. Most such measures are, however, likely, either directly or indirectly, to cut into the sort of maximum corporate profitability demanded by finance-dominated capitalism. There is no such thing, for example, as a maximally efficient worker with slack, time to burn, and sufficient money in the bank to refuse unreasonable demands at work.

Efforts to keep past and future from distracting from the urgent task of turning one's life around now do not, however, in Christianity deplete the present moment of its time dimensions in the way relations to the present within finance-dominated capitalism do. Turning to God is a life task, something that should characterize one's life as a whole—one's entire past and entire future—even if such a task needs to be resumed every day as if from scratch. In maximum contrast to the short-term time horizons of profiteering in finance-dominated capitalism, here one's time horizon is exceedingly long. In acting now one imagines oneself, for example, brought before God's judgment seat after death. At every moment one is encouraged to assess the profitability of one's own life, so to speak, from its end in the eyes of someone, God, with the capacity to see the whole of it to its very depths. One imagines oneself engaged in such a task, moreover, in the company of all those similarly concerned—those who came before, the blessed dead, and all those who will in future go to make up the communion of saints before the world's end. One holds them in mind now, as if they existed concurrently with one's own efforts at the moment to make one's life over in God's image: one sings together with them, for example, before the communion table. In so doing one participates in the present in God's own awareness of time, an awareness with the capacity to hold together at once, to form into a simultaneous whole, the entirety of such past, present, and future efforts at God devotion.

Aware of the whole of earthly time in these ways, one is thereby temporally oriented, placed within the flow of time, for all of one's preoccupation with the present moment. One knows where one stands with reference to past and future insofar, for instance, as one is helped by the example (both good and bad) of all those who have gone before and insofar as one hopes in turn to aid in similar fashion all those who will come after. One is placed in that moment of temporal transition between the whole of the past and the whole of the future.

Far from being depleted or empty, the present is pregnant with significance because in a certain fashion—by way of its God reference—the whole of time is present within it. This is not a "see the world in a grain of sand and eternity in an hour" kind of meaning-filled instant (as in the thought of William Blake).[45] Present in one's perception of the moment, the whole of time is not narrowed down here to a single precious point but rather retains its expansiveness. The present moment is not, in other words, made precious in and of itself by way of the fact that the whole is somehow found concentrated within it to form its very own particularity, or because it assumes such a particularity only from the standpoint of the whole that includes it within itself as an essential part. Instead, the present takes on its significance because it contains the whole of time offered in a nondivisible and co-present way in the God to whom one is oriented. Whenever God is present, as God is in the grace than enables one to turn to God, God is present as a whole rather than simply in part. What God contains, the whole of times at once, becomes thereby ours as well in the present. This a remarkably replete present moment, filled with an eternity that when present is entirely so.

The present moment may have no duration. It may fly by, as Augustine suggests and finance-dominated economic transactions do their best to confirm, from the future into the past with such speed as to have no extent.[46] The present moment of turning to God retains nonetheless a quality that opens it up to much more than itself, to times far beyond itself, to God's own eternity. However little or much one experiences of God, however little or much one understands of what one is experiencing, it is the whole of God that one is so experiencing or knowing. What one experiences in the moment is in that sense always complete and entire as it stands and cannot be added to. The fulfillment that would come from turning oneself completely to God in the instant could not be improved in quality even were that moment to be infinitely extended.[47]

A life suffering from a kind of unintegrated dispersal is collected together, unified beyond its own capacities, by attention to a God beyond it. One's life does indeed form a series of disconnected presents in that the same task of turning the whole of one's existence to God has to be repeated, taken up again, at each succeeding moment; those moments do not, for reasons discussed in the last chapter, build on one another. And such a task must be repeatedly assumed with proper attention to differences in circumstance that, especially in finance-dominated capitalism, are liable in themselves to form a disconnected sequence of simply one thing after another: at one moment, for example, one needs to figure out how to properly express one's devotion to God with a good paying job, and at the very next moment one needs to figure out how to do so without one; at one moment one needs to establish how one's devotion to God can be expressed as a mortgage broker with a potentially lavish lifestyle (probably by quitting!), at the next moment—after the financial crisis hits—how that might be done while working as a carwash attendant and living out of one's suitcase on a friend's couch. However much one's successive presents otherwise form a disorganized jumble, one is always trying to do the same thing, turn one's full attention to God, in ways that no change in circumstances can thwart. One's fundamental project does not change across such an otherwise disconnected series of presents; one retains a single point of orientation that unifies one's life as a whole.[48]

It is the unusual character of the object of attention that enables one to do this. Unlike the specifics of present circumstance, what it is that one is attending to—God—never comes and goes. One is never simply attending to the rapidly changing present itself—the opportunities it offers for profit—in the way finance-dominated capitalism encourages one to do, with a simple reactivity that would break up one's own life into bits in conformity with the dispersal of such changing presents. One is instead looking in a discriminating way at every present moment, examining it for the opportunities it offers to direct it beyond itself, to something that, unlike itself, never changes. One is looking through every present moment to something that (unlike monetary profit) is not itself part of the same ever-changing, unpredictably volatile mix, something with an absolute value, therefore, in that it is not dependent on the ups and downs of a passing present.

The cure for disorienting dispersal—a life of distraction in which one is tossed hither and yon, to and fro, by the winds of fortune—becomes in this way the same as the cure for simple temporal distention, the constant passing of time—from future to present into the past—in which nothing is ultimately retained and everything returns to the nothing from which it came: the cure is time's reference to the eternal. In the beginning, as Augustine says, the heaven of heavens

> through the rapture and joy of its contemplation of God, ... has power to resist the propensity to change, and by clinging to [God] unfailingly ever since its creation . . . transcends every vicissitude of the whirl of time. . . . At no time and in no way does it shed its mutability . . . but being always in [God's] presence and clinging to [God] with all its love, it has no future to anticipate and no past to remember and thus it persists without change and does not diverge into past and future time.[49]

When the effects of sin are dispelled and one returns to what creation was meant to be, every moment, in what became through sin a passing time of disconnected sequence, will find itself repeatedly referred, moment by moment, in an equally direct fashion, to a God who never changes. All such moments will thereby be collected together in coherent fashion, not with reference to one another but by way of a reference they all share to the same, invariably present God.

All the disconnected moments of one's passing life would be collected together, one might say, in every single such moment of perfect Godwardness, so that rather than passing away, such a moment would expand in duration to become a "day that never ends." Glorying in God's own eternity, one would come to enjoy oneself a never-ending day, a day in which one remains forever present to oneself, aware of oneself, in God. Whatever goes on to happen in one's life and however short one's remaining time, by remaining in God one would remain forever aware of oneself, present to oneself, in God. The longest day—the longest present self-awareness—might in this way be granted to one on even the shortest day of one's death: today you are—right now at the hour of one's death—with me in Paradise.[50]

The mere attempt now under conditions of sin to collect one's life by way of its God reference relaxes concern about one's own abilities to keep it all together and thereby dispels anxious efforts at self-collection in the present. Unlike, say, a Stoic effort to escape self-dispersal in a volatile environment, here it is God—the object of one's will—rather than the ability to unify one's own will successfully in every present moment that makes the difference.[51] It is not so much the unwavering constancy of one's own life project that assures one's ability to step back and collect oneself, whatever happens, but the constancy of that ever-compromised project's object: whenever and however—in whatever fashion—one turns to it, it remains. The two—one's self-project and its object—are not convertible here in the way they are for Stoicism, because here the self is not fundamentally providing itself with the resources necessary for unifying the passing present. Those resources come from elsewhere, from the object that orients one and is nothing like oneself. Contrary to anxious efforts to achieve a finally consolidated will, here one expects repeated failures of attention through distraction and forms of divided desire, and believes one has fundamentally nothing to fear from them. Grace remains untouched for all that, and holds out to one, as ever, sufficient power to turn.

The world's turbulence, its own random dispersal, in fact gives one nothing to fear in the present, in the way a worldview like Stoicism, which throws one upon one's own resources, suggests it does. One need not fear, for example, the way such turbulence threatens to take out of one's hands the ability to control the direction of one's own life; one need not fear that turbulence even if it has demonstrated its power in the past to get the better of one, tossing one to and fro. One's past failings hold no terrors; one's present efforts to devote oneself to God can be resumed without impediment, enabled by God's grace as they are, whatever one's own proven imperfections.

Nor need fear of the future prompt in the present anxiety-filled efforts to hold onto the moment at hand in a self-protective attempt to keep even the little one has from passing away. If the never-surpassed state in this life of constantly reinitiated conversion is any model for how to approach the present, believe that this moment of anxiety-filled insecurity too will pass, and with it all that one has attempted to secure for oneself in extraordinarily adverse circumstances. Especially given the indignities of the very little allowed to one by finance-dominated capitalism—and the injustices attendant upon trying to have more—such a passing of the present is to be welcomed. A mindset of self-protection, resigning one to the present order out of fear, is to be replaced by one of eager openness to an unheard-of future to come.

5
Another World?

Within the financial markets that dominate the current configuration of capitalism, the future becomes of special concern because of how likely it is to differ significantly from the present in ways that will either make or break one. One might be riding high but one is very much aware that the stock market could tank in the future, taking one's job and savings with it. Even if the future is not in one's control, best then to prepare for it. Precisely because things are likely to change drastically and have an enormous impact on one's fortunes, it pays to be prudent, to turn attention to the future, to anticipate what is likely to happen, and to take appropriate action now to make the best of things, come what may.

As we shall see, however, finance encourages people to approach such an anticipated difference between present and future in ways that, ironically enough, close up that difference. Its methods for dealing with the likelihood of quite impactful differences between present and future have the effect, in other words, of collapsing the present and future into one another, at least at a second-order level. One does not expect the future to be like the present, but one nevertheless expects the future to be no different from present anticipations of it. The future is quite likely to be significantly different from the present but in ways that financial instruments for dealing with that difference lead one to expect can be reliably forecast.

In order to profit from the difference between present and future, or at least to prevent it from doing any harm, one employs financial instruments that collapse the future present—that is, what the future will turn out to be—into the present future—that is, into the present view of the future.[1] Confidence about the ability of such financial instruments to manage for one's economic benefit what is likely to be a drastically different and quite impactful future depends on considering the one—the future to come—to be the equivalent of the other, the present view of the future. By virtue of such a collapse of future into present, the future one anticipates loses its capacity to surprise; the future to come simply reduces to the future it makes sense to expect given present circumstances. Those circumstances themselves become a kind of self-enclosed world, as one learns to hope for nothing more from the future than what the given world's present limits allow, what it is reasonable to expect from within them, assuming their continuance. Present circumstances come to constrain imagination of the future, in other words, by setting a rigidly circumscribed boundary of possibility that cannot be crossed. It becomes thereby easier—as Fredric Jameson famously quipped—to imagine the end of the world than to imagine the end of capitalism.[2]

Financial Focus on the Future

If circumstances were not at all in keeping with the volatile ones of finance-dominated capitalism and one expected the future to be just like the present, one would have little reason to give the future much thought. When people think the future will simply bring more of the same, the future garners no special attention in and of itself. The future is likely, it is assumed, to be nothing more than an extension of the present, and for that reason what one already knows about the present provides all the information one needs to have about the future. It becomes of much greater interest per se the greater the future's anticipated difference from the present, the more likely such a divergence from present circumstance is thought to be, and the more consequential its possible effects. If the future is probably going to be very different from the present and to have a significant impact on one's fortunes, it is a good idea to turn one's attention to it.[3]

These characteristics of the future that make it of interest in its own right may be typical of modern life generally; they attend the recognition of the significant future impacts on both individuals and society of free human decisions about what the future should be. The social relations that form us for better or worse are ours for the making; one therefore has no reason to assume they will be the same in the future as they are now. The organization of human life could indeed be radically different from what it is now; whether it will be or not awaits the contingent choices of human agents.

Social forms could be made very different from what they are now if one cared, for example, to try to make them significantly better; modernity, indeed, sees all sorts of experiments in social improvement. Social forms have varied considerably in the past and elsewhere. It is always possible, here and now, for them to become markedly different in the future, depending on what it is that people decide to do about them, in order to remedy their defects or augment their benefits. Just to the extent that people choose to do things differently now, those social relations will in fact be somehow different in the future. Present decisions inevitably have future effects—they make a difference and exert an influence (to some degree or other), whether or not those future effects are what one intended, whether they unroll according to plan or not.

It is not just, then, that things could always change in the future in ways that have the potential to significantly impact one's livelihood for good or ill. Modernity surely has no monopoly on unexpected windfalls and precarious fortunes. In whatever time one lives, one can always be sure that the future will be very much unlike the present in certain respects: one is alive now but inevitably at some point will be dead. What comes with modernity is the recognition of the dependence of changed fortunes on human decisions with an impact on the future. Rather than simply finding oneself in favorable or dangerous circumstances irrespective of one's own choices, one puts oneself in the position to either benefit or suffer a loss in the future depending on what it is that one decides to do now. By virtue of deciding to do something now, one gains the possibility of benefiting from such a decision in the future; if, however, things do not turn out as expected, one's present decision makes one liable to future loss.

It is the future that will tell whether the choice one makes now was the right one or something to regret; one therefore has reason to anticipate what the future will be when deciding what to do now. Only the future, however—and not present anticipation of it—will have the final say; one has to wait to see how things turn out in order to judge the propriety of one's decisions in the present. This need to wait is at least partly a consequence of the complexity of social circumstances under which decision-making takes place. Complicating decision-making in the present, in other words, is the awareness that everyone else is making decisions with some degree of impact on the future too: their doing so, in ways one cannot control or even thoroughly ascertain, makes the outcomes of one's own decisions, for both oneself and others, uncertain. In making decisions now one cannot in short—because of this kind of social uncertainty—count on the future being the way one anticipates it being.

In trying to decide what to do now one often therefore imagines oneself looking back from the future at a past that is one's present and hoping any such decision will not have proven to be a mistake. The future in this way emerges in present decision-making "as a kind of advance memory."[4] One wonders now from the perspective of the imagined future about the benefits and losses that one's own decisions will have helped to bring on oneself. In all these ways a future distinct from the present becomes a peculiarly salient matter for present consideration under conditions of modernity.

These characteristics of the future that make it a distinct subject matter for concern may be found in modern life generally, but they are exaggerated to an almost unheard-of degree in finance-dominated capitalism.[5] Economic decision-making certainly does routinely exhibit the sort of concern for the future that I have been suggesting is typical of modernity. Like perhaps almost any decision in modern life—from a personal decision about whom to marry to a policy decision by a state legislature to ban smoking advertisements—one wonders, too, whether one's investment decisions will turn out to be good calls from the perspective of the future. One knows one is taking on certain risks and the potential for certain future benefits in virtue of such decisions—the decision to buy a stock, take a job, sign those loan papers—and only the future will tell whether those decisions were good ones or not. The future reveals that one cannot get the job one has gone into debt to train for, because everyone else made the same decision and the competition for such jobs is now incredibly fierce. The future stock market crash reveals how terrific a decision it was to switch all of one's assets into bonds the year before. Because so much is riding on what the future holds, it becomes important to imagine the future now when making economic decisions.

But finance-dominated capitalism presents far more than a typical instance of a modern concern for the future as such because of the fact of highly volatile economic circumstances upon which one's fortunes now depend. Big changes in economic circumstance become a regular, everyday occurrence. And those changes have a direct, and quite significant, bearing on one's ability to make a profit or assume a loss—in great part because financial assets are nothing more than claims on future income.

Everyone knows, for example, that the valuation of stocks on a stock exchange is unlikely in the future to be the same as it is at present, given, for one, the dependence of such valuations on changing demand.[6] The price of a stock goes up and down depending on how many people want to buy it from moment to moment. The mechanisms for making a profit on those markets indeed count on the likelihood of there being significant differences between present and future values, the bigger the better. If the stock market were to remain flat, no one could lose money by buying and selling there, but no one would gain anything either. The greater the difference between future and present values, the bigger the potential for greater profits—on the part, for example, of those market participants whose investments correctly anticipated the direction of future fluctuations in stock prices.

The financial markets that set the terms for the economy as a whole are, moreover, not just routinely volatile but very likely at some point or other to be extremely so, with enormous economic consequences. It is this ever-present possibility of extreme volatility that especially heightens every one of the characteristics of the future that make it an object of distinct concern.

Assets traded on financial markets (for reasons to be discussed more fully in a moment) are liable to swing wildly in value, both up and down, and with great speed in tandem with shifts in market sentiment that often seem to turn on a dime. Those potential swings in valuation are indeed so extreme that they have the capacity to wipe out the gains of a lifetime overnight or more than compensate in a single day for decades of steady, small losses. Even if the extremes are rare—stock values do not plummet everyday—extreme swings are nonetheless likely to happen at some point. Stock markets are prone to booms and busts and will almost always, because of their magnitude, have a huge impact on the economy when they do.[7]

Financial markets, for all the reasons we have been discussing, have a special interest in the future. They foment a concern about what the future will bring, since so much is riding on that. But they also turn attention to the possible difference between the future and the present, because that difference is a prime source of profit—or loss. Furthermore, they promote consideration of the potential difference between the future one anticipates and what the future turns out to be; if the future is significantly different from what one expects and has planned for, the financial consequences, given market volatility, could very well be devastating.

Indeed, one might say that financial markets are so interested in the future that consideration of the present for all intents and purposes simply collapses into concern about the future. The future—in all these different respects—becomes an all-consuming preoccupation in every present decision. Whenever one seizes the day, to make the most of every present moment before it is gone, it is to the future that one is looking. When deciding whether to buy a stock, for example, one need not be particularly concerned about the present profitability of the company issuing it, apart from the bearing of that on the real questions of importance: What is the future value of this stock likely to be (as that is determined by its future price on the stock market)? By how much is the value of this stock likely to go up (or down) in the future? And what if the future proves such anticipations of future value and degree of possible future fluctuation to be wrong? How likely is it that the future will prove judgments about it now to have been mistaken?

The present price of a stock typically, indeed, builds into it answers to all these future-oriented questions; the present price in this way simply becomes a calculation based on answers to such questions about the future. Present value collapses into discounted future value; present price simply reflects, for example, a stock's anticipated future value (among other future-oriented considerations). Financial assets amount to claims on future income, and therefore the character of those future income streams in volatile financial markets—the likelihood of their increasing, by what margin, and how quickly—goes to establish present value.

Thus, no matter how presently profitable the company issuing it, the present price of a stock depends on whether market participants believe its value will go up in the future and by how much. This is because market participants are not buying a stock to reap company dividends that add up incrementally over the time the stock is held; in that case, present company profitability, if it at least held steady, would make buying such stock profitable, assuming one remained so invested over the long term. Market participants instead are typically buying with the hopes of selling purchased stock to someone else willing to pay more for it—ideally, much more for it—in the future on the exchange. If buyers do not anticipate anyone being so willing, then they will not purchase the stock. If market participants believe the price is unlikely to go up by much—because, say, this very profitable company lacks the capacity to be much more profitable in the future—the present price will reflect that fact. Demand for the stock will be low, even if the company issuing it is enormously profitable at the moment, and the present price of the stock will also therefore be low, as a result of low demand for it.

If present prices are to price in the future, in all the relevant respects—that is, price in likely future value, likely degree of variation in future value, and likely accuracy of both these anticipations of the future—the future itself will have to be priced. The future must, in other words, be subject to calculations that provide it with a monetary value if present prices are to reflect it. How much, for example, one is willing to spend on a stock depends on such calculations. If the future cannot be assigned a number, the present value of a stock cannot be given a number either.

It is the way financial markets address this need to price the future reliably that ends up collapsing the future into present estimations of it.

Given the very volatility that makes it such a preoccupation in present investment decisions, one might think no reliable way exists to price the future; the future is just too unpredictable. Because the value of assets on financial markets can vary so widely, indeed swing wildly from one moment to the next, who knows what price such an asset will fetch tomorrow, let alone over any extended period of time?

Simply because of its futurity, the price of a financial asset at a later time does not yet exist. By definition, the future is nothing until it arrives. But much more than this, the future price of an asset on a financial market would seem to have no determinate value—and therefore nothing to measure—ahead of present purchasing decisions made about that asset. Because of the way prices in financial markets are set by demand, future prices are to a significant degree determined by the number of people who now decide to buy, or not to buy a stock (based on anticipations regarding its future value). Future value simply awaits such decisions in the present as their cumulative effect.

These problems might be insurmountable if pricing the future into present value required one to know in advance what the future at any particular point might bring. But, fortunately, that is not the case, and other options for pricing the future appear to remain.[8] One cannot reliably predict what the price of a financial asset will be at time T in the future, but one might still think one could reliably predict the range of its possible values then. Calculations regarding the future routinely shift accordingly away from simple future forecasting—which is widely recognized to be impossible at any significant remove—to consideration of future variability. In order to determine what one should pay for a financial asset, all one needs to know about the future—indeed, all one can get—is reliable information about the range of the swing in its value, up or down, that is likely to occur over the period of time one holds it. One needs, in short, to be able to predict the asset's volatility in future with some certainty. The price one is willing to pay in this way comes to depend on a kind of risk assessment. The more risky the asset, because of greater volatility in comparison to other assets, the less one is willing to pay for it, unless such risk can be compensated—by the possibility of outsized gains.

But how can one calculate volatility? If prices are volatile in ways that make them unpredictable, is the volatility of those same prices not unpredictable too? Prices of a particular asset may have exhibited a certain range of variation in the past but why assume the likelihood of that same range of variation in the future? Past price is not a good indicator of future price—that is admitted—but past variation is nevertheless taken to be a good indicator of future variation. Only indeed on such an assumption—of continuity between past and future—can future volatility be made calculable. And in this way the difference one expects the future to make is lessened; one is confident that one already knows what it can hold, within a reliable range.

Indeed, if one were genuinely basing expectations of the future on past market behavior, that past would disrupt confidence about one's ability now to predict the future—whether it be particular values or the degree of their variability. If the past were really one's guide, one should conclude that the future is no more predictable now—in any respect—than it was in the past.[9] The past's future—that is, the future as it appeared from the standpoint of the past—proved to be unpredictable, a surprising shock; the present's future—that is, the future as we now see it from the standpoint of the present—should be similarly unpredictable. It is only with the benefit of hindsight that what others failed to expect in the past appears a likely result, completely unsurprising given what came before. Past market crashes, for example, always seem to be almost inevitable, financial assets having been bid up well beyond any sustainable level. Even if the exact moment could not be foretold, the crash had to happen at some point or other, it now seems. But that is exactly what was not generally apparent then or so many people would not have continued the buying frenzy in such assets right up until the point of complete market collapse.

It makes sense to think this sort of continuity between past and future volatility will prove an exception to the market's usual incapacitation of prognostication only if one assumes prices exhibit a random walk around a supposed standard or correct value and can therefore be plotted on a Gaussian bell curve.[10] In that case, markets are something like games of chance with known probabilities of outcome. The probabilities of heads or tails are known with certainty by virtue of the stable properties of the coin to be flipped. Extreme variations in the number of heads or tails that appear sequentially are predictable on that basis—one can calculate the probability of the unlikely event of one thousand tails in a row—and eventually, given enough tosses, one can be certain that the number of heads and tails will even out. But financial markets are not like simple games of chance, for one, because future prices are not independent of past ones (and for another, because the true or proper value of financial assets is not primarily a reflection of what is outside market dynamics themselves). One coin toss tells one nothing about the next. Future prices in financial markets, to the contrary, have everything to do with past prices, especially in the recent past. The high demand, for example, that recently bid up the price of a financial asset is itself taken to signal expectations of future upward price movement, and in that way feeds even greater demand and with it higher prices.

Or, when continuity between past and future in market volatility is assumed, it is often thought to be predictable in the way the always surprising fact of one's death, when it arrives, is subject to strict actuarial calculations by way of statistical probabilities from accumulated past data. Using data about the actual past frequencies of such events, one can calculate with great reliability how many people will die and how many houses will burn down in a particular town in a given year, and thereby the likelihood of deviations from the norm that will even out over the long term. But market values are far more unpredictably volatile; it has, indeed, been historically demonstrated how occasional extremes in market volatility all but wipe out any hope of return to some supposedly normal value. For example, declines in housing values in many markets fail to rebound after a crash no matter how steady the population looking for housing and valuable the housing stock itself—gorgeous designer kitchens, incredible square footage, and so on. Although nonetheless rare, complete market routs are simply far more common than simple statistical probabilities would predict.[11] This is in part because the past data employed in such calculations often does not extend far enough back into the past to include the last time a rout happened. But it is also because markets seem to be like towns periodically subject to die offs, everyone seemingly threatened with death at once (of apparently natural causes rather than simply because of unusual external events like natural disasters or enemy invasions), even though the preceding stability in death rates over an extended period of time would give one no reason to expect as much.[12]

However ill-advised the confidence in predicting the character of future volatility, the simple fact of that confidence means the future itself can remain unknown while allowing for pricing oriented to it. All that matters for present pricing of financial assets is a current, backward-looking market consensus about future volatility; all that must be susceptible of calculation for purposes of present pricing, in other words, is the way future volatility looks at present to most market participants.[13] Whether for well-founded reasons or not, people do in fact think they can give the likely future variability of financial assets numerical values. There are widely accepted formulas, indeed, for making calculations of value at risk (such as the Black-Scholes formula). It is simply the fact of such a widespread practice that provides the basis for present pricing.[14]

That sort of basis for present pricing holds across the board, whether it involves anticipations of future volatility specifically or not. Actual present prices in general reflect what most people at present think the future will be like, since that to a great extent determines present demand. For this reason, one can put a number on the current value of a stock—price it reliably—if one can put a number on how many people presently think a stock will go up or down by a certain amount within a particular future timeframe. It is the present calculation of the future that in this way becomes measurable; the future itself, as any direct matter for consideration, recedes from view. What one is willing to pay is simply determined by judgments about present anticipations of the future or what I term (following Niklas Luhmann) the present future. The future present—what will actually turn out to be the case in the future—is not really at issue. The possibility that it will be radically different from what everyone now expects it to be can simply be set aside in present evaluations of what a financial asset is worth.[15]

Indeed, present anticipations of the future do not just help establish the present value of financial assets in this way; they have an enormous impact on actual future values.[16] For just this reason it would seem to make sense to forgo worry about the possibility that present predictions could prove mistaken; they cannot be mistaken because they help in great part to bring about the very future they predict.

Present anticipations amount, in other words, to a kind of self-fulfilling prophecy, in virtue of the way future prices on financial markets are determined endogamously, that is, by internal market dynamics fueled by demand. For example, the more people who buy a financial asset today because they anticipate, for whatever reason, its rapid future rise in value, the more the price will in fact rise in the future due to that heightened demand.

Anticipations of price rises do not merely help to bring about what they seem to predict; they also have the capacity to feed on themselves, in a kind of self-generating spiral, up or down, because of the same market dynamics. Present anticipations of the future are more than confirmed as a result. By virtue of their simply having them, people's hopes of future profit in making present purchases are routinely exceeded.

In other nonfinancial markets for goods and services, increased price lowers demand. (If the price of peanut butter doubles overnight, demand for it will decline precipitously.) And lowered demand then leads to lower prices. (The price of peanut butter will have to decline to get people to resume their old buying habits.) On financial markets, by contrast, present price increases, fueled by increased demand, tend in and of themselves to foment even greater demand in the future, thereby ratcheting up future prices all the more. This sort of feedback occurs because, irrespective of any independent verification of what warrants it, an increase in present demand, and the price increase that accompanies it, are taken to be a signal of market confidence about future price increases, thereby spurring increased buying and helping in and of itself to elevate prices further.

In both these ways—because anticipations of the future in financial markets help create what they predict and easily generate self-propelling feedback loops—the future present tends to collapse within financial markets into the present future in fact. The future regularly turns out in reality to be just what market participants expect it to be or even to exceed their hopes.

Until of course that point where the future fails to conform to expectations. By way of such market dynamics, prices of stocks, for example, are eventually inflated well beyond anything that might be justified by actual increases in corporate profitability across the board. Prices then abruptly reverse course, with the likelihood of a feedback loop of a negative sort now kicking in. Prices precipitously decline in self-propelled fashion to a level well below what that very same assessment of corporate profitability would warrant. Even if it is not much of a factor in setting present prices on financial markets, financial operators are, indeed, well aware that the future may not turn out as anticipated. They must know, even if that knowledge is not at the forefront of their consciousness, that the models used in the present to price future volatility (for example) could prove to be inaccurate, and that, if and when they do prove to be so, the consequences are likely to be devastating—just because that possibility has not been factored into present prices. No one expects that a two-thousand-point drop in the stock market on a single day could happen in a million years (if calculation of that likelihood assumes market prices follow a bell curve, in which the likelihood of an event happening dramatically decreases with the degree of its divergence from the average); that very fact makes such a drop, if and when it comes, all the more devastating, because people have been buying stock with an eagerness predicated on failure to see that very drop coming. Everyone has been investing more in the market than was prudent, bidding prices up way beyond sustainable levels, and in the process making huge, devastating drops for everyone all the more likely.[17]

Many of the major innovations in financial markets—financial markets in derivatives—are designed to protect against this very possibility that the future will not turn out as anticipated. For example, should one fear the price of an asset will rise in the future beyond what one will want to pay, one can contract now to pay a predetermined price at that future date. If the price at that time happens to be more than the contracted price, one saves the difference between the contracted and actual future price. If the actual future price turns out to be less than what one agreed to pay for it then, one loses the difference between the two and has to pay just that much more than one would otherwise have had to. But at least by taking out such a futures contract, one protects oneself from the possibility that future prices will be higher than one is willing to pay. Or one can pay now simply to have the option of paying a specified price at some future time. One need not exercise the option unless the actual price in the future is higher than the contracted price when the time rolls around. The price might turn out of course to be lower than what one has the option of buying it for then, making the contract of no use, but purchasing such an option at least protects against the possibility of having to pay more than the contracted price.

While they are in this way predicated on the possible difference between expected futures and actual ones, these contracts—futures in the one case, options in the other—nonetheless have to be priced themselves. How much is one willing to pay for the security of being able to pay in the future no more than what one would now like to pay? Or, conversely, how much does one require to be paid for being a counterparty to such a futures contract, for assuming, that is, the risk that the target price of a futures contract will be much lower than what one could actually have sold that asset for in the future? To answer such questions and come up with a price for options and futures contracts themselves, one needs to have a way of reliably forecasting the likely range of future prices up or down for the assets such contracts concern. Indeed, only if a high level of confidence exists concerning the accuracy of the probabilities assigned to future variations in those asset prices within a certain range can these derivatives be priced. The sort of calculations about future volatility discussed earlier are for this reason most directly relevant to derivative markets in particular, because the risks and possible rewards of volatility are what such derivatives directly concern. These derivatives are specifically designed to deal with volatility and, for that reason, require the ability to price it. As discussed before, however, reliably pricing future volatility entails the collapse of future presents into present futures; that collapse returns with a vengeance in the pricing of derivatives, even though the difference between the two is what gives rise to the need for derivatives in the first place.

In short, the probabilities of variation in future prices within a certain range need to be reliably calculated for the derivatives that concern such future price variations to be priced themselves. If markets in these derivatives are to exist at all, those probabilities cannot simply remain unknown (however much the wild swings typical of financial markets might give one reason to think they are). But reliable calculation of those future probabilities is only possible, as we have seen, if the future is to a very significant degree like the past, if, that is, past volatility provides good evidence for future volatility. For this reason, the possibility that the future will disappoint predictions about it once again disappears from view; such an idea drops out of consideration, impelled by the need for present pricing of derivatives.

Indeed, even apart from what follows from the need to price them, derivatives are all about taming the ability of the future to surprise, depleting its capacity to be anything other than what one wants it to be. Derivatives, for example, allow one to make money off the differences between present and future, whatever those differences happen to be, whatever their degree, large or small, and whatever their direction, up or down. Whatever the future brings, it is therefore to one's liking. The potential of the future to cut into profits can be tamed by financial instruments that offer to do that for a price.

So, for example, if one's investments will turn a profit only if the purchased asset goes up in value in the future, one can take out a derivative contract that guarantees a pay off in case the value declines. Either way, irrespective of what the future brings, one wins. Derivatives in this way allow one to hedge against the failure of any simple directional bet; because of volatility in financial markets such directional bets are often likely to be wrong.

Derivatives amount in other words to a kind of insurance against the downside risks of volatility in financial markets (with those downside risks being assumed by counter-parties willing to do so in exchange for present profits taking the form, in effect, of insurance premiums). But unlike ordinary insurance contracts against, say, fire or flood, which allow one to benefit from things one hopes will not happen, derivatives do not require ownership interest in the assets insured. This allows one to turn potentially hefty profits from even minor market volatility. Because one pays only the costs of the contract itself that insures against asset value decline and need not have bought the underlying asset that is so insured, one's potential profit in case of that decline is pure profit. Derivatives, in other words, amount to insurance contracts on other people's lives and houses (and become thereby simple bets). The payoffs need not offset any actual losses in the way an insurance payout can offset the loss of one's home, leaving one still with a loss but with a much smaller one than would otherwise be the case. Rather, one simply enjoys the payoff free and clear (minus the costs of the contract itself); almost any payoff, no matter how small, has the capacity to be positively lucrative.

In general, derivatives promise to tame the future's capacity to limit choice.[18] Despite the fact that once it happens one will not be able to do anything about it, derivatives purport to make the future a source of open possibility rather than constraint. In the future a certain asset will go for a certain price, but taking out a derivative contract now means one will not have to pay that. One can pay in the future whatever one freely decides now one would like to pay then, by taking out a futures contract. Or leave the matter open by buying options. In these ways derivatives work like money—at least apparently— to expand the range of future possibility. One does not know what the future will bring, what one will need or want. It is best then to keep one's assets in cash, rather than using up that cash in purchases now, presuming to know what one's long-term needs and desires will be and thereby foreclosing them.

Derivatives hold out the promise that the future will never get the best of one. By employing derivatives one can be ready for anything the future might hold. Whatever might happen, one retains the possibility of turning a profit. Derivatives promise, in sum, to close off the future as a possible source of life disruption, as anything with the capacity to throw one's life off balance.

They promise to do this by virtue of their ability, first of all, to make the future into something already anticipated and dealt with proleptically. The future is brought into the present and dealt with now so one will not be taken off guard; one can neutralize the disruptive potential of the future by folding it into the present. Like the Stoic penchant for imagining in the present the worst thing that could possibly happen in order to gain practice in composure, one can use a derivative to imagine the worst possible future scenario, given one's present asset allocation, and take steps now to offset its effects then, should the worst happen. Buy, for example, a derivative now that will pay off big in case such a disastrous future scenario comes to pass. Like the present-oriented point of the Stoic practice of anticipating one's death—the point is to train one now to be an athlete of the unexpected event, the master of all that could befall one—the point of anticipating the future becomes in great part its consequences for developing the appropriate habits of derivatives purchasing in the present, a kind of prudence enacted through financial planning.[19]

Or one can do an end-around whatever the future in fact will bring by employing derivatives that amount to a kind of refusal to commit to particular outcomes—by employing options, for example. In that case, one buys derivatives that themselves seem to instantiate free and open possibility, as a way of countering any downsides from a future one does not even try to predict. Derivatives would promise to defuse a potentially disruptive future in much the way that people honing their flexible capacities are hoping to cope in a volatile job market: they are ready for anything by keeping their options open and not putting all their eggs in one basket. Again like Stoicism—in this case, its practice of refusing to choose anything (except virtue) without reservation so as to avoid disappointment—

derivatives, options in particular, would permit the refusal of any unreserved choice about matters whose realization the future could hinder.[20] I would like this asset I own to rise in value in the future, but if the future excludes that possibility, that is okay with me too. I will exercise my option to limit my losses. I commit myself to a certain hoped-for future in virtue of my present investment decisions but only with the reservations represented by the derivatives I also take out now to hedge my bets, should the future turn out otherwise.[21]

Unfortunately, in the case of financial markets at least, such promises of a defanged future turn out to be spurious, for reasons I have already intimated. The future to come is not likely to conform to present anticipations of it, in great part because those anticipations are based on calculations that assume a much greater continuity between the future and the past than is warranted. Somewhat ironically, the more people are convinced of derivatives' capacities to tame the future, the more imprudent they become, taking more risks than they should—indeed, given market feedback loops, taking ever more risks the more that other people take them—so that it becomes all the more likely that the future will bring catastrophic surprises. Fomented by the very derivatives that promised a future of open possibility, that unanticipated catastrophic surprise now closes off all possible options: the circumstances, for example, are now so unstable that no one knows what such derivatives are worth anymore—they cannot be priced—or they become so expensive, now that such failure is proved by events to be much more likely than previously thought, that no one can purchase them. When that catastrophic surprise comes, the financial instruments designed to assure an open future become, moreover, useless. In the event of a major market meltdown, for example, the losses incurred among the counter-parties who assumed the risks of such a downturn become too extensive to cover the claims against them. There simply is not enough money available to pay those claims in the very circumstances those financial instruments were supposed to help investors weather.[22]

Christian Hopes for the Future

For all the Stoic influence on Christianity, Christians typically do not, like actors in today's financial markets, take steps to neutralize or master a disruptive future, if by that future one means their ultimate transformation to come through the gift of Christ's Spirit—resurrected life. This is not simply because they are confident of that future's beneficent character: Why take steps now to prepare for a future that will be absolutely delightful? The future Christians expect retains a strongly negative flavor of potential disruption, something whose effects it would therefore make sense to try to nullify prospectively, and not just because Christians sometimes think that future might include damnation for some. Even a purely benevolent end—universal salvation—retains a highly negative cast to the extent such a future will tear us away from what we remain in and of ourselves, sinners. The more sin is part of us, who we are, that with which we identify, the more the transformative effects of grace are felt in fact as a kind of torture, what rips us away from everything we otherwise are and love improperly.[23]

One might "master" these rupturing effects to come if one were less a sinner: one might make the end less painful by preparations now that take the form, for example, of moral self-improvement. But Christians who believe (as I do) that the character of Christian lives before the end will always warrant confession and repentance—and who have a modicum of

honest self-awareness stemming from such a constant peniten-
tial practice—typically do not expect those efforts ever to come
to much in this life. There is too much empirical disconfirma-
tion proving premature Christian claims to righteousness in
this life. While Christians are confident that the gift of the
Spirit in Christ is sufficient to enable their thorough reformation, sins, though now forgiven, remain surprisingly salient for
whatever reason in most Christian lives. It is difficult, in short,
to support expectations of achieving the end in this life from
the evidence of just how well things have been going so far.
Indeed, in a host of at least apparent ways, the world does not
seem appreciably better after Christ's incarnation than before
it. While they may be united with Christ in faith and love for
him, Christians have arguably so far made no especially great
moral progress toward that new manner of existence made
possible in Christ. Their record of moral achievement gives
them little with which to boast when compared to observant
Jews or righteous unbelievers. The Holocaust, for one, has
certainly humbled any such pretensions.

But even assuming a significant degree of moral and
spiritual advance in Christian lives up until now, it ever remains
the gift of grace. This dependence on grace is what fundamentally rules out considering any such advance a self-propelled
process furthered by mere efforts at self-reformation. Indeed,
what lies at the root of any achieved transformation can never
be simply transferred to the human in the form of new created
powers of self-mastery: human beings remain dependent on
the very Spirit of Christ within them for any ability they display
to lead life differently. The uncreated grace of the Holy Spirit
itself always lies behind any created graces that take the form
of new human inclinations to be God-devoted and loving toward one's neighbor. This continuing dependence on what lies

beyond the human is all the more evident from the ultimate end of such transformative processes. Unlike moral righteousness, eternal life or the enjoyment of God's very own life is not in principle anything one could gain, or even incrementally approach, by way of human powers per se, no matter how improved they might one day become in their own right.

In contrast to Stoic and financial tactics of willing with reservations whatever the future could adversely affect, there is, moreover, no possible way of doing an end-around that ultimate end that Christians expect. All other possibilities at such time will be foreclosed by God. In much the way that death forecloses them, there will be no "keeping one's options open," no room for maneuver, at the end of days, and therefore no point in taking steps now to try to assure that.

In part because they do not take any of the sorts of steps taken in financial markets to master it, the future that Christians expect remains as radically different from the present as it could possibly be, short of not being a future suitable for human creatures. In general, Christian responses to such a radical difference between present and future, unlike those encouraged by financial markets, do nothing to close up the difference.

Christians do make the future a special object for attention in its own right for the general reasons financial markets do. Christians expect the future to be quite different from the present way life is lived, and they expect that what the future holds will have an enormous bearing on their fortunes. Considerations of the future cannot be collapsed into considerations of the present, therefore; knowing about the present way of the world will not tell one anything much about the future that will one day come. The future requires its own special attention.

If anything, the general, already heightened reasons for considering the future in financial markets are even more heightened in Christianity. It is hard to imagine a future of more momentous import, bringing with it, as it does, the prospect of either eternal life or eternal torment. And Christians expect resurrected life (at least) to be as different as it could be from the life one lives now, still typified by moral and physical corruption; one needs indeed to go through death—both figuratively and ultimately literally—to get to it.

One will remain the finite creature one is, however radical the ultimate transformation of human existence itself, simply human potentials finally perfected in the end. But one's whole manner of existence will nonetheless be changed from the ground up, insofar as one will one day come to live off the very life of God already one's own in Christ. One will not simply have that Spirit of Christ for one's own, as one does now, but one's whole life will transparently manifest that fact, in ways that cannot be anticipated beforehand.

Although obviously of incredible interest because of its enormous significance for human fortunes, most Christian theologians for this reason remain circumspect about their abilities to describe what is finally to come. While always tempting—will our bodies be ethereal? perhaps spherical? and so on—such descriptions remain in their most important respects purely speculative. The character of our ultimate future state is often admittedly unknown, simply unimaginable, because it will be as radically different from the present as it can be, short of being a simple replacement for it. On what basis could one imagine it, given that it represents no simple extension of the finite human creature's own potentials but a literally God-infused life?

Even if the character of the life one will be living at the end of days remains unknown, Christians feel little doubt about the fact of resurrected life to come. Christ's coming has assured that. One can be certain, on the basis of what Christ has accomplished, that one will one day be resurrected too, despite having no real idea of what resurrected life will be like. Because predicated on confidence in Christ, this certainty about the future does not depend on any calculations from data supplied by generalizations about the character of human life past and present. Such calculations, as we saw in the case of financial markets, would bring back into the picture significant continuities between human life now and in the future. Christians, in short, have no need to close the gap between present and future, to insist on continuity, in order to be sure of that future.

If one does the math (so to speak), the probabilities of the future Christians expect can indeed be next to nothing using such data. Christ's second coming, and the general resurrection of the dead that will attend it, may be no more likely now than Christ's incarnation was then—that is, not at all likely, as unlikely as anything could possibly be, given the character of human life preceding them both. Keeping the earlier unpredictable surprise of Christ's advent in mind, Christians may in this way be unusually resistant to the hindsight bias that so commonly afflicts risk assessment in financial markets. Christians, I argued in chapter 2, typically tell stories about themselves and salvation history that stress just how unpredictably surprising the future looked from the standpoint of the past. They do not typically use retrospective stories about the past to smooth over discontinuous jumps in previous sequences of events but to highlight them. Looking for lessons from the past, they therefore have little reason to think the future will be any less surprising from the standpoint of the present than it was from the standpoint of the past.

Moreover, what Christians hope for does not become any more likely to the degree progress in manifesting the grace of

Christ in human life has been achieved (assuming, for the moment, there has been significant progress). It is not the amount of progress so far that gives one hope of final achievement of a perfectly grace-manifesting life but the power of Christ's own working even now through his Spirit. The likelihood that the future will see such a perfectly grace-filled life simply does not increase or decrease with the evidence so far—or ever—suggesting human success in manifesting that grace.

Indeed, according to Christian understandings of it, what the future will bring in the end is simply not the sort of thing that can be subject to means/ends calculations at all. It makes no sense to think, if I do this (behave morally), then that (eternal life) will become more likely, in much the way, if I invest in the stock market, my gaining 10 percent a year will be more likely than were I to invest in bonds. Being moral cannot be the means, within any means/ends calculation, to life in God, because it is itself the anticipatory effect of life in God now. What enables one to be moral now is the same thing one hopes will be fully manifest then—life in God. Life in God is something one enjoys now—what Christ has already accomplished—and cannot, then, be the consequence of actions taken to get it. Rather than it being the consequence of our actions, those actions are themselves the consequences of it: the life in God secured for us by Christ is what we are drawing upon now to live differently.

For this reason, while the future remains enormously important to Christians, they often fail to make it the direct object of future anticipation, if that means anxious attention to what the future might hold given the present state of the world. They are, in other words, like Søren Kierkegaard's boat rower, getting on with the task of leading life differently at every moment, with backs turned to the direction of movement.[24] Turning one's attention directly to the future to come in order to assess one's progress or lack of it is to make that future the subject of calculations of more or less, and therefore fundamentally to misunderstand the way to get there. Turning to look directly at the destination one hopes to reach does not get one there any faster; doing so simply hinders one from rowing in the way one should. Because it is powered by the very presence of Christ's Spirit within one that makes possible transformations in human life beyond the scope of human capacity (whether sinful or otherwise), arriving at the destination involves a kind of jump from one whole manner of existence to another—from the life one lives now in the struggle against sin to a life fully transparent to God's own life. Believing one gets to that new life primarily under one's own steam, as a function of the rowing, one turns back to see how far there is to go and in the process mistakes the goal for something brought closer by human success, something such successes approximate, a matter for incremental approach along a purely created axis, simply more of the same. One thereby—ironically—delays that future's coming by substituting a different sort of future for it altogether; anxious about arrival, that turning threatens to make it all the more unlikely.

What I have been arguing for here—the unmitigated, radical character of the difference between present and future in Christian thought—has indeed been widely recognized and has often been made the subject of hostile critique (by Marxists, for example). According to that critique, the radical difference between now and then proves purely compensatory for Christians, reconciling them to the very conditions that such a stark difference between now and then helps them to deplore. Do not worry if there is nothing to be done now to better those horrible conditions; things will all be made right in the end, with those awful circumstances now reversed by means not of one's own making. Or, even worse, even if there is something that could be done now to improve things, do not make the effort, leave the matter to God.

Christian hopes do not prove compensatory in this way when, as in the theological position I have been developing, the future to come is in the most important respects pulled into the present. The grace that is necessary to change things radically exists and is at work in the world now, providing human beings with everything they need to live life differently. There is, therefore, a way for us now to get from here to there because the motor of that change is as much ours now as it ever will be in future—that motor being life in Christ. The future to come in this way funds the struggle for realistic proximate futures in the present. Drawing on that grace of God, one should do everything one can now to manifest it in the character of the life one leads. No reason not to start with what the world at present would seem to make a realistic possibility. Even if the past provides little grounds for expecting such efforts to be any more successful now, what impels these proximate efforts, and gives one hope against hope for their success, is the same grace of God that underlies one's ultimate hopes. Present hopes for the near future are directly fed in this way by far-off future hopes, which will only come to fruition in the eschaton.

This sort of pulling of the future into the present does not, however, like a structurally similar move in the pricing of financial assets, have the effect of lessening the difference between present and future. The future that is present now remains disjunctively present, one could say. It remains, as the very grace of God, everything that the sinful life surrounding it is not; indeed, as the very presence of God, it remains absolutely different from everything created that surrounds it. Although it

funds realistic, proximate hopes for change, what one ultimately hopes for—the ultimate hope that drives all these
proximate ones—is another world entirely.

That future state of the world to come, in which transparency to God will be perfectly realized, remains an absolutely
other world in that only God and nothing about the world's
own tendencies and trajectories makes it possible. Rather than
being the realization of this world's own latent future possibilities, the power of God fully manifest in that future world is
what presently pulls this one toward it, in ways that therefore
ensure a never-filled gap between this whole world and the
next.[25] Despite this never-filled gap between the whole world
of continuing struggle against sin and the next without it, this
other world has been entering into every present moment in a
disruptive way so as to form an otherwise impossible historical
trajectory of history's apparent losers, a historical movement
made up of all those who, swimming against the stream of their
times, never seemed to get anywhere. What will finally come
will establish once and for all what could never be predicted:
that their efforts were not in vain, were not for nothing, that
their efforts to bring in another world did not, as they appeared
to, come to nothing, vanish without consequence.[26]

What are the lessons to take away from all this? I am not
suggesting that the Christian account of the future I have just
developed provides an alternative model for treating the future
within financial markets, as if it would make sense to try to
imitate Christian approaches to the future within those markets,
as if the character of those markets could be improved, for
example, if Christians themselves acted differently within them,
according to their own quite different ways of approaching the
future. Instead, I am applying to financial markets as a whole
the Christian approach to the difference between present and

future. I am suggesting, that is, that the financial approach to the future is part of the present world to be left behind, a world to be repudiated in all the very basic ways it counsels people to relate to themselves and others, in favor of a whole new world to come that will be as different from this world as possible. But which one?

6

Which World?

Each one helps the other, saying . . . "Take courage." The artisan encourages the goldsmith, and the one who smooths with the hammer encourages the one who strikes with the anvil, saying of the soldering, "It is good"; and they fasten it with nails so that it cannot be moved. But you, Israel . . . whom I took from the ends of the earth, and called from its farthest corners, saying to you, "You are my servant, I have chosen you and not cast you off"; do not fear, for I am with you, do not be afraid, for I am your God; I will strengthen you, I will help you, I will uphold you with my victorious right hand.

—Isaiah 41:6–10

Do not fear . . . I will help you, says the Lord. . . . Now I will make of you *a threshing sledge, sharp, new, and having teeth.*

—Isaiah 41:14–15

I am about to do a new thing; now it springs forth, do you not perceive it?

—Isaiah 43:19

In ways I now address more explicitly, this book has been exploring the new work ethic of finance-dominated capitalism and has been attempting to dissociate Christianity, in particular Protestantism, from that ethic. Like the spirit of capitalism that Max Weber describes, the new ethic of finance-dominated capitalism remains a work ethic. Indeed, finance-dominated capitalism (as we have seen in chapters 2 and 3 especially) is structured to require, whatever the nature of the work, maximally strenuous exertion of all of one's capacities as a person. This work ethic is also a time ethic—like the old one was but now in heightened form.[1] One should manage time as one would any financial asset, to make the most of it, to put it to profitable use in the most efficient and cost-effective way possible, losing no time, wasting no time, leaving no time undercapitalized, as it were.

What remains to discuss—the specific topic of this last chapter—is the way a finance-dominated work ethic is individualizing in highly moralistic fashion. Finance-dominated capitalism uses a variety of institutional means to single out individuals and render them accountable for their own fortunes, the bearers of either praise or blame. Economic success or failure becomes one's individual responsibility, revelatory of who one is as a person. Moralized evaluation of individual success or failure figured prominently in the old Protestant work ethic and now reappears in exaggerated form within a finance-dominated work ethic.[2]

Economic success or failure in that old religious ethic was deemed indicative of one's fundamental individual character—reflective, that is, of the particular standing before God that defined one in religious terms, success being a mark of election to salvation, failure a sign of exclusion. One was singled out by God for either salvation or damnation, and one's economic success or failure revealed one's final destiny as an individual too: one became individually responsible for it. Hoping to confirm one's salvation by the character of one's economic activity, one worked hard as capitalism demanded—in order to gain economic success and in that way distinguish oneself from others, not just economically but religiously.

This way of relating to oneself and one's economic fortunes has now been shorn of the religious support it required in capitalism's early days. Trying to distinguish oneself economically from the vast majority of those less fortunate within finance-dominated capitalism has become highly motivating in its own right, given simply the economic stakes involved. The economically elite—the economic elect, one might say—are very few, and the difference between the economic top and bottom can be extreme, amounting to a kind of economic heaven in the one case (more money than any one individual could possibly spend apart from an interest in space travel) and damnation in the other (drudgery in exchange for low pay at best, along with a life of constant worry).

Such a moralizing way of relating to oneself now, moreover, has everything to do with how one relates to others. While the previous Protestant work ethic certainly did tend to extend a moralizing self-understanding to the understanding of others—their success or failure was their own responsibility too—the economic lives of other people were their business. Each person remained in fundamental respects alone with God, in both the religious and economic aspects of life; no one else had anything fundamentally to do with it. In similar fashion, many aspects of the spirit of financial capitalism could conceivably remain formative simply of one's own self-understanding, implications for relating to others remaining to a great extent undeveloped. To the contrary, the aspect of the new spirit of capitalism to be discussed now has, as we shall see, an enormous, very direct significance for how one relates to others; it indeed incorporates and sums up the social dimensions of all those other aspects.

Within finance-dominated capitalism, an individualizing moralism with respect to oneself presupposes and implies specific ways of relating to others. For example, relating to oneself in a moralizing fashion is fomented by the way finance-dominated capitalism structures relations with others in competitive, winner-take-all markets. And in so relating to oneself, one shores up or reinforces that very same competitive structuring of human relationships.

Because it forms not just individual persons but their relationships, this aspect of the new spirit of capitalism works to set up a whole social world. This is the world, I hope to show, Christians have reason to oppose. How Christianity brings together relations to oneself with relations to others establishes, I suggest, an entirely different, other world that fundamentally calls this one into question.

Individual Responsibility and Competitive Relationships in a Finance-Dominated Work Ethic

Several features of finance-dominated capitalism coalesce to heighten the demand that persons assume individual responsibility for what they do and suffer. For example, finance-dominated techniques for worker management typically enforce individual attribution of responsibility. To get the most out of every worker, remuneration is calibrated to individual effort. Performance pay, in short, becomes the norm, as an efficiency-maximizing tactic.

Wage levels are not set across the board on a shared basis. They are not set, for example, according to the general sort of job performed, with differences in pay within a single pay grade determined by a possibly wide-ranging criterion such as seniority. Wage levels are not even established on a case-by-case basis by group performance of particular tasks, every member of the group rewarded together, with the same bonus, say, for a job well done. Despite the fact that jobs require teamwork and are often organized through a network rather than a linear production line—all of which hampers assessment of individual productivity—every effort is made to evaluate individual performance and match individual pay to it.

This difficulty in assigning individual responsibility for work done in teams and across networks creates significant internal tensions for management strategies typical of finance-dominated workplaces. Even using computer technology, employers often find it hard to determine exactly who was responsible for what, even though such calculations are necessary to determine performance pay. Teamwork and networking make it very easy for individuals to capture recognition and rewards for work done by others; team leaders or upper management responsible for simply setting group targets are therefore always tempted to take credit for more than what their own efforts contributed to outcomes. Charges of inequity in so-called recognition capture often crop up among critics of finance-dominated capitalism who note a near systemic failure to live up to capitalist norms of equitable merit pay.[3]

Finance-disciplined state policies that cut costs of welfare provision are another major way demands for individual responsibility are enforced. Debt-strapped states that make paying off sovereign debt their priority lack the revenues to meet expectations of welfare provision. At best they do lip service to such expectations by making it easier for individuals to take on that responsibility themselves. For example, rather than providing universal education, states make it more affordable via tax credits for people to buy private schooling for their children. Or rather than establish publicly funded hospitals, states simply ensure individuals have sufficient information to make informed choices among private providers.

At worst, states renege on responsibilities for welfare provision altogether. To save costs and put revenues to more efficient use, states push welfare functions off onto private, market-based providers and throw individuals onto their own resources in purchasing whatever furthers their health and happiness from such providers.

The mechanism here is very similar to that used by finance-disciplined, often debt-strapped companies for the purposes of streamlining internal management and reducing costs. Rank-and-file employees are forced to take on functions previously performed by middle managers, whose ranks have been decimated in cost-cutting schemes. Aside from setting performance objectives, upper management does not coordinate worker activities from outside those activities. Instead of amounting to a sort of planned economy, operations internal to the firm now take on the character of a free market in which workers act on their own recognizance to organize themselves most efficiently. In so doing they open themselves up to a kind of individual liability; when things go wrong, charges of mismanagement fall on them rather than on the company, which has relinquished responsibility for direct management.[4]

Similarly, in finance-disciplined states, responsibilities for addressing risks to the well-being of the population (illness, unemployment, and accident, for example)—risks previously assumed by the state—are now shifted onto affected individuals themselves. States require such individuals to secure themselves against threats using private means, such as by purchasing individual insurance. Social insurance—a social sharing of risk—is thereby replaced by demands for individual prudence. If one does not prepare for the worst and position oneself to make the most of whatever hand one has been dealt, one has only oneself to blame.

Personal responsibility for individual decision-making can retain a social dimension. For example, there is a social dimension to being prudent and taking out an individual insurance policy; private insurance pools the risk in that the money used to compensate unlucky individuals comes from the accumulated premiums of those not similarly affected. Such coverage also places individuals within a group of similarly situated others, using statistical averages. Nevertheless, all forms of insurance short of unrestricted state-supplied welfare are always significantly de-socialized. The pool of funds for compensating loss is not gathered from society as a whole but has restricted parameters; for insurance purposes one is compared to only a small subset of the population made up, say, of smokers of a certain age and sex like oneself. Coverage is moreover conditional and not guaranteed; payment into the pool is necessary for coverage. One cannot be indigent, then, but must have private funds, generated typically through remunerated employment.[5]

By demanding individual responsibility, state policies like these work directly against the poor, leaving them defenseless, because, by definition, the poor lack private means to secure themselves. And the more that poverty puts them at risk, the more insurance typically costs. Indeed, costs to those at greatest risk are much higher now absent the sort of mandatory universal coverage only the state can enforce. Insurance costs to the weak and vulnerable are no longer subsidized by the young and strong; individual costs are simply proportionate to individual risk and therefore the highest for those most in need of protection. Moreover, private insurance typically protects only against loss to capital assets. In insurance terms, one's life, for example, has no specific value apart from its money-making potential. Lacking capital assets one either cannot get a policy at all or one with only a very small payout.[6]

Ample state provision of social insurance remains only for those with the power in market terms to force the state to assume responsibility for the losses they have incurred. Too-big-to-fail financial firms are the major recent case in point. States giving priority to creditors rather than to welfare programs typically still seek legitimation from the economic prosperity their policies supposedly foment. Individuals can fall by the wayside without putting much of a dent in the gross domestic product; big financial firms threaten to take everyone with them.

A welfare state hollowed out by financial-market discipline promises to individualize profit: smaller government means keeping more of one's earnings for oneself. Those earnings increasingly will not be socialized in the form of taxes for redistribution to others via welfare payouts. But the flipside is that downside risks will not be socialized either. When things turn ugly, one is on one's own.

This is supposedly for one's own good—and the good of the wider society—according to the usual ways of thinking that support such policies. Welfare creates a moral hazard by encouraging a culture of dependency that saps people of their initiative and willingness to work. The greater the social support, the less people are inclined to become entrepreneurs of their own lives. According to this line of thought, one owes it to oneself to assume responsibility for oneself in ways that make one less of a burden on others. Individuals become much more efficient in the management of their lives, more skillful managers of their capacities and resources, of their human capital, when forced to bear the costs of failure themselves; they thereby become less likely to ever need state help.

The idea that individuals act rationally in their own interest—that is, according to a means/end calculation of how best to pursue their needs and wants—combines here with the idea of persons as entrepreneurs in the development of their own personal capital.[7] According to such an account, not just the state but the individuals comprising its population have an interest in furthering their health and economic well-being. Who knows better what they need and want and how to get it? Best to leave it to them. Having to assume personal responsibility for failing to achieve their ends, as the state now requires, individuals make more efficient and profitable use of their own resources.

Because having to take individual responsibility for failure incentivizes a population to make productive use of individual capital, states no longer aim, as earlier welfare states once did, to produce a risk-free society, a society in which no one fears, say, loss of employment. State policies that aim to diminish welfare provision indeed increase the risks individuals run, on the assumption that such risks are not always bad. Risks are good in that they focus the mind and make action more intentional; risks provide opportunities for creative entrepreneurship. Rather than securing their population against risks to health and well-being, states leave it up to individuals to decide what risks they are willing to run in a risk-filled world, a world organized through state policy to foment the precarious character of individual fortunes.[8]

When offered, state welfare provision also tends to individualize persons. One no longer has a right to welfare as a citizen, for example. Instead a citizen is only able to claim benefits by virtue of a kind of individual contract with the state. Benefits come only to those individuals agreeing to make a return for them—not in money (which people in need of welfare do not have) but in the currency of their future actions, so to speak. In return for benefits welfare recipients must, for example, look for work and accept any job offered, no matter how poor the pay.[9] Welfare benefits become in this way a sort of loan, obligating recipients indebted to society by accepting such payments to future performance of the sort of behaviors a society considers payback.[10]

The same targeting of individuals within contractual exchange is increasingly found to an even greater degree in actual loans for the purchase of consumer goods or homes. An individual credit score, summing up one's entire credit history in a single number, determines exactly how much money a lender is willing to provide and at what interest rate. Those determinations are thereby person-specific rather than a matter of general demographics. What I am given and what I am required to do in return are not simply a function, say, of my being a white professional woman interested in purchasing a condo in New York City but are peculiar to the specific person my particular economic history establishes me to be. In similar fashion, employment agreements within finance-dominated capitalism are highly individualized. An employer agrees to hire at a pay level reflecting the specific aptitudes and achievements of that individual; pay thereby singles out the employee as an individual by placing her exactly where she belongs in the ranks of other employees, as just that particular person with a hair more qualifications and previous work experience than the employee paid a bit less.

In all these ways, states concerned to further the economic well-being of their citizens try to actively enlist them in the effort, by getting them interested in maximizing their own capital and minimizing their own risks. Individuals then come to do the work for such states. Previously, citizens became targets of interest for states not in their individual specificity but under the guise of statistical averages established by actuarial techniques. Framers of state policy were concerned about the effects of state policy on individuals on average: how many people were likely on average to give up smoking, if smoking advertisements were banned and taxes on cigarettes doubled? Through monetary incentives and penalties expected to have statistically significant effects, government tried to shape conduct without acting directly on individuals in ways that might interfere with their free decisions.[11] Finance-disciplined states reneging on welfare obligations now enforce in effect individuals' direction of their own lives by way of the very actuarial techniques previously used by states to direct them. States get people to do of their own accord what aligns with state interests.[12] Assuming responsibility for one's well-being because the state has left one to one's own devices, one is inclined, apart from any special government inducements, to try to stop smoking (for example) simply because of the high statistical probability it leads to cancer.

Given the risk shifts typical of finance-disciplined states, one cannot depend then on help from others when one fails. But neither in finance-dominated capitalism can one depend on others to advance. This is not primarily because finance-disciplined states reneging on social insurance are also inclined to renege on positive, empowering welfare provisions designed to give people a leg up—childcare, educational benefits, subsidized transportation, and so on. It is because the structure of markets in finance-dominated capitalism prevents people from profiting together: within finance-dominated markets, one person's gain has to mean another person's loss.

The use of relative rather than absolute benchmarks for assessing worker performance is one such institutional means. An employer does not determine, for example, that three hours is the minimum time necessary to perform the job well (an absolute standard of performance), with everyone matching that time or going below it getting a bonus. Instead, bonus-worthy performance demands surpassing one's coworkers' performance (a relative standard, in which excellence is established over and against what other people do). The standard for excellence being relative, if someone by superhuman effort manages to turn in a time of two hours, while everyone else comes in at three, that single employee could very well enjoy a bonus for excellent performance alone.

The use of bell curves in management decisions about employee pay and retention heightens this same effect—with the end, once again, being efficiency maximization. To be safe, an employee has to come in above the curve—that is, above the average level of worker performance. Going below it means a pay cut and puts one in line to be fired. But the curve shifts—the average level of performance goes up—as all workers try harder to beat the current average, and as workers who fall below the average are progressively let go, leaving only the very best workers behind. Just because the performance average constantly ratchets up, at some point, unless one can keep pace, one is likely to fall below the average and be let go. Everyone is potentially under threat from everyone else in such a pay and retention system; gains made by coworkers can only portend one's own downfall.[13]

Across the board, measures taken by finance-disciplined corporations to maximize profitability prevent workers and employers from profiting together. Thus, even when making outsized profits, corporations cannot risk sharing them with employees by raising wages. Doing so would only cut into company profit margins and thereby threaten the price of company stock. In general, stock market discipline inclines companies to maximize company profits at the expense of others, often (as we have seen previously) by fobbing the costs of doing business onto others. So, for example, company profits depend on workers keeping up with new technology, but the costs of the required training fall on employees themselves, who have to undertake it on their own time.

Derivatives along with secondary markets for them—indeed, secondary markets for financial assets of all kinds—have structurally similar features that keep people from profiting together. Especially when not hedging risks incurred from actually holding assets, derivatives amount to simple bets against another party. Just like in a casino, the side betting wrong supplies the winnings to the side betting correctly, and this precludes both winning.

In the case of ordinary insurance against ownership risks, if I lose my bet and never need the insurance, I also win—because, for example, my house never burns down, which is what I feared and tried to hedge against by taking out fire insurance. I lose the money I paid in premiums, but, besides still having my house, I also gained the peace of mind of protection against loss. Profits from insurance against ownership loss are for this reason always to some extent mutual.

Where derivatives suppose no ownership interest, when one loses, one loses to someone else, pure and simple. Rather than gaining protection against risks faced in owning the underlying asset, buying the derivative initially created all the risks I ever ran: for example, the risk of losing money from the price decline of an asset I do not even own. I have thereby set myself up for a thoroughgoing loss to a counter-party.

The internal dynamics of secondary markets for financial assets might suggest to the contrary that market participants win and lose together. For example, the more people buy a stock, the more the price goes up, to every buyer's profit. And the more people sell, because, for example, the company issuing that stock failed to meet its quarterly profit target, the more the price goes down, with every owner of the stock seeming to suffer together from the decline.

Market participants are, however, profiting or losing to varying degrees, and this dispels the impression of shared gains and losses. If one buys before everyone else, one profits far more than the person who jumps in and follows the crowd later on, at the top of the market. Only the former makes a killing; the latter makes next to nothing. Earlier sellers are spared the losses of those who come after them and indeed contribute to those losses by pushing the price lower.

Run-ups and sharp declines in price are in this way closely linked: run-ups in price foment later sharp declines. Feedback loops push prices beyond sustainable levels. Decline then sets in, with similar feedback dynamics pushing prices lower in just as exaggerated a fashion. Timing the swing between boom and bust is where the real money promises to be made in volatile markets like this.

Ideally, one sells at the top of a run-up in a stock's price before everyone else does and the stock's price plummets. If one manages to be among the lucky few, one takes the whole pot; before the market plummets, one takes the money from the rest who bid up the price. Market dynamics producing market swings in this way lead to very few big winners. Everyone wins together from a run-up in asset prices until the value created by everyone's investments is captured by the few exiting the market before the general stampede. Winning together only sets up eventual huge wins by a minority of players. It is a kind of fattening up of the turkeys before they are slaughtered and eaten by other market participants.[14]

Winner-take-all markets that produce few winners become, indeed, increasingly common throughout the economy, often aided by computer-mediated product provision.[15] When goods and services are supplied by way of the internet, a single provider often comes to dominate the market; every purchaser attempting to minimizing costs eventually chooses that one provider with marginally lower prices and higher quality products relative to all the others. When companies subcontract or outsource rather than organize and pay for company functions in house, the same supplier can end up servicing a number of different corporate customers. By reliably undercutting the price and raising the quality just a tad more than others, this supplier can push others out of the market altogether. A similar winner-take-all effect arises from company mobility, the ability and willingness of companies to move operations to low-cost production sites. When all companies try to minimize payroll costs, even a few cents' difference in average pay from one area of the world to the next can spur a mass migration of companies' operations there. To the extent one can call them winners (given the rock-bottom wages paid), people in that area of the world become the sole "winners" in the labor market for such jobs.

In general, with value in finance-dominated corporations determined by relative position, few people can be winners. Everyone scrambles for the same few positions at the top, and the fortunate few who make it take all the winnings. The management tactics for bonuses and retention we looked at earlier have this character. Eventually, only best and brightest remain, their now unusually high relative remuneration being paid for by the savings from having fired everyone else.

Everybody cannot win in labor markets managed in this way because what every worker is after is a positional good, whose value is established only in besting others. The ability to see over the heads of others in a crowded theater is a simple example of a positional good with such effects. I can only enjoy that good alone, by standing up while everyone else remains seated; their standing up too threatens to make my doing so worthless. I would have to go up on tiptoe to gain any advantage, with everyone else then following suit. The eventual outcome of all this jockeying for position is a single winner—the tallest person in the room.[16]

Finance-dominated capitalism across the board does nothing of itself to encourage the idea of people profiting together, since profit-taking is usually not dependent on other people making money too. We discussed this before in the case of loans: because they are immediately sold on secondary markets, one is not particularly concerned about whether loans are used by borrowers for their own profit. That profit is not supplying the funds to pay creditors back; buyers of the loans on the secondary market are. Should borrowed money be used unwisely, later holders of the bond, not the original lenders, are the ones left holding the bag. Similarly, finance-disciplined corporations need not worry if workers do not profit when the company does, and consequently have no money to buy what their labor produces. So long as paying them so little has the effect of increasing profit margins and raising the value of company stock, there is little to worry about. Presumably somebody has to have enough money to purchase what the company sells—maybe best just to count on people profiting from the purchase of company stock.

Profit-taking via derivatives is similarly indifferent to whether anyone else is making money; that is in great part its point.[17] Indeed, profits can increase the worse off other people are. For example, in hard times higher interest can be charged for loans; the interest-bearing bonds that collect and repackage such loans for sale on secondary markets become thereby more attractive to investors. Or one shorts the market on an economic downturn in order to profit from it. One borrows stock to sell to others with the intent of buying it back and returning it to the original lender at a lower price later; one nets a profit from a decline in the value of the stock, the bigger the decline the better.

At the root of this evident inability of people to profit together in finance-dominated capitalism lies the fact of heightened competition. One cannot depend on others to help one profit because finance-dominated capitalism forces one to compete with everyone else in all the avenues it offers for achieving profit.

State and corporate tactics to single out individuals seem intended to put everyone into a competitive relationship with everyone else. One is turned into an individual in the eyes of the state or corporate headquarters, solicited as an individual responsible for one's own fate in order to assure such competition. For example, the corporate use of relative rather than absolute benchmarks for worker performance means not just that one is assessed individually rather than as a member of a group (which could also happen using absolute benchmarks), but also that one is judged over and against other group members in a kind of forced competition. The more obviously individuals are singled out by employer modes of assessment, the fiercer the competition with coworkers. Thus, when one has done a fine job as part of the team that pulled in a huge client for the firm, one is not patted on the back by upper management at a party celebrating the work of the whole team, nor does one's regular monthly salary now show an increase as silent testimony to one's especially good performance. Instead, one is called individually into the office of management at the end of the year when everyone's bonus is calculated and provided with a very large, one-time windfall that tempts one to make an immediate show of it in a luxury car purchase. This sort of spectacular individualizing of employee performance very obviously has the effect of ratcheting up competition among the workforce; it leads everyone to focus more intently on the positions they hold vis-à-vis others, in particular at the end of the year, as they jockey to maximize the credit that is their specific due.[18]

States would similarly seem to be ensuring the competitive social circumstances required by capitalism. Contrary to the laissez-faire policies of liberal states, finance-dominated ones no longer seem to assume that economic competition is a natural development, managed best when left alone to run its own self-regulating course according to specific economic laws that politically motivated intervention could only affect adversely. Competition is no longer simply presumed to come into existence on its own, with government entering the picture after the fact to remove external impediments to its proper functioning. Instead, according to a now neoliberal way of looking at things, competition needs to be actively encouraged by government policy in order to be set up and remain in place. State policies that cut back on social services and make people assume responsibility for themselves are one major form of encouragement. By such means, government policy itself promotes the idea that each person is an individual enterprise, existing among a multitude of other such enterprises, all competing to maximize their capital for maximum profit at minimum expense. The highly competitive social circumstances that oil finance-dominated capitalism have been made the business of the state.[19]

Individualizing policies encourages competition, then, but that competition in turn only feeds the need for individual responsibility. It is in great part because one is in competition with everyone else that one must fall back on one's own resources to get ahead. It is either you or them.[20]

Capitalism is always predicated on competition, but the finance-dominated form of capitalism has peculiar features with unusual effects. Competitive markets in finance-dominated capitalism are, first of all, much more extensive than markets have previously been, indeed maximally extensive to include every possible participant. So, for example, in the labor market, one is in competition for open jobs not just with members of the local community but potentially with every worker on the planet. And as job requirements target flexible capacities rather than specific skills, anyone can replace anyone and no one is indispensable. Much the same goes for exchange markets. Companies can lose market share to any company, anywhere, in the same line of business. Indeed, given flexible, reprogrammable equipment, any company anywhere, even if not currently in that line of business, could come into the market and capture market share.

Competition within finance-dominated capitalism also tends to differ qualitatively from that of earlier capitalist markets—by fomenting direct individual-to-individual rivalry. Take the labor market. Workers have always been in competition with other workers for jobs but not directly so. The judgment about the relative qualifications of the various applicants took place behind applicants' backs, by remaining the decision of a third party, the hiring company. Competition with other applicants was mediated, in other words, through one's individual relationship with the company. Moreover, one is not now hired on what is expected to be a permanent basis in virtue of what one has brought to the job. Instead, one needs to prove one's value to that employer continually. One is rated constantly relative to other employees or even relative to people out there somewhere whom a company can simply threaten to hire or outsource the job to. One is permanently at risk of being fired and needing to be hired again. Furthermore, the standard for assessment no longer exists outside all of this jostling for position in any fixed fashion—in the form, say, of a job description. The standard is simply what the other people one is competing with make of it. For all these reasons, the value of the labor one hopes employers will recognize is nothing one can achieve simply by oneself. What one has made of oneself, independently of others, is not what differentiates one from them; it does not provide the prior basis for distinction from others as a kind of unintended byproduct. Instead, one brings about what makes one distinctively oneself in the very process of actively differentiating oneself from others in a quite directly competitive contest with them.[21]

A similar change occurs in commercial markets for the exchange of goods and services. These have usually been organized in ways that protect against any direct, agent-to-agent competition that might foment rivalry among producers buying and selling to one another. Avoidance of possible hostilities was indeed among capitalism's early selling points. Participants in these exchange markets do try to sell for as much as possible what others would like to buy as cheaply as possible; there is a kind of competitive conflict of intent here between buyers and sellers. But it is mediated through impersonal prices in ways that eventually bring about agreement: I offer you ten dollars, you counter with twelve, and we meet in the middle at eleven, in a thoroughly amicable fashion. The realization of different productive specialties within a highly developed division of labor ensures as well a complementary dependence among producers for exchange rather than conflict-generating rivalry. We are not all trying to sell or buy the same things. I am not trying to sell to you what you already have and are trying to sell to me, but what you lack and need. I am not trying to buy from you what you also feel in need of and are trying to buy, rather what you have that I do not.

Of course, I might want to buy what you also want to buy and you get there first, making such purchases more difficult for me. Likewise, I may want to sell to others what you also want to sell to them, your managing to do that before me leaving me in that much more difficult a sales position. But no one is wedded to what they want to buy or sell in commercial markets; they are doing it for the money. Given that the ultimate agenda in capitalist exchange markets is to make money (rather than enjoy the things traded), if what I want to buy has already been purchased, I can simply choose to buy something else with a similar profit-making capacity. And if I cannot sell what I would like to, because the market has already been cornered, I can simply switch product lines (facilitated by post-Fordist techniques).

Moreover, this sort of competition—within the pool of buyers, on the one hand, and the pool of sellers, on the other— is also impersonally mediated by the market and its pricing mechanisms. I know of that competition and react to it because of the way supply and demand fluctuates and with it the prices for goods, and not by personally concerning myself with my fellow buyers or sellers. If everyone else wants to buy what I want to buy, I will see that in price hikes and limited store inventories. If companies competing with me for market share undercut my selling price, I will see that in a drop-off in demand for my products. Participants in well-functioning competitive markets do not have the power individually to sway them— these are aggregate effects on supply and demand and pricing. Everyone therefore remains subject to the market as a sort of external mediator of relations with other market participants; in taking the actions one does, one is reacting to the market rather than to any particular competitors.

Secondary markets for financial instruments do not, however, work like this. For example, huge individual bets, aided by leverage, do have the capacity to move the market. Smaller investors betting the wrong way are thereby directly affected by what individual big players do. Their investments can be rendered worthless by a single big player flooding the market with sell orders, for instance. In a similar fashion, very large corporations made large by financial means can have an enormous effect on exchange markets. Given their already huge market share, their lowering prices could enable them to bankrupt especially smaller competitors singlehandedly. Most very large corporation have for this reason an at least tacit agreement not to compete with one another by lowering prices. While prices remain steady, they compete with one another by lowering costs—for example, in a race to the bottom to lower their respective payroll expenses.[22]

But the main reason secondary financial markets become directly competitive is the lack of external mediation.[23] Trading on a stock exchange, for example, is not simply a matter of independent individual assessments by traders of what underlies the value of the stock (say, the profitability of the company issuing it), an underlying value external to the market in that it could be established apart from the buying and selling of stock on that exchange itself. The price of a stock, instead, directly reflects opinion about the value of the stock itself (rather than the company)—that is, consideration of the likelihood of the stock itself (for whatever reason) rising in price because of greater demand for it on the exchange. The going price of a stock need not even aggregate what people individually have assessed the value of that stock to be; the price reflects the general state of opinion about that value, with the price market participants are willing to pay converging around that consensus. Because consensus in opinion makes the price of a stock rise (or fall), the behavior of market participants is determined by deliberative processes in which everyone is trying to assess what everyone else thinks. The opinion of others thus becomes a direct concern for everyone.

Moreover, in contrast to ordinary exchange markets (where some want to sell what others want to buy), everyone wants what everyone else wants in financial markets; they share the same objects of desire and therefore strive to keep others away. In these secondary financial markets, buyers and sellers change positions with one another constantly to a single end: they all want the price of what they have bought to go up, and to cash out at the height of the market. Rather than have a shared interest in the same investments, they all have a shared interest in the liquidity of those investments (which is what a secondary market is designed to provide).

One might think the abstraction of such a shared interest would lessen the potential for rivalry: one is not, after all, fighting with others over the same potentially scarce material objects of enjoyment. But exaggerated forms of direct rivalry remain. All market participants cannot sell at the same perfect time—there would be no one left to sell to. Thus competition is over the timing of that exercise of liquidity, which can make or break buyer or seller. Everything depends on gauging correctly what other people will do, in order to beat them to the punch.[24]

Because these markets are so unusually competitive, one cannot expect help from other people of their own accord, help that would come at their own expense. In a finance-disciplined corporation, for example, my helping you get a bonus—by, say, performing for you some urgent task that, being at home with your sick child, you are unable to address yourself—just makes it all the more likely I will not get a bonus. But there is also nothing about the organization of these markets that would lead others to help you even inadvertently, that is, by way of some impersonal, unintended market mechanism.

In virtue of the so-called invisible hand, commercial markets can coordinate the independent activities of people producing goods for exchange to their mutual benefit, whether or not those producers have any intent of benefiting others. I am trying to make money by selling you this bread and not deliberately doing so to ease your hunger, although that may be the unintended effect of my trying to profit from such a sale. Typically, producers of marketable goods are simply self-concerned and have no intent to help others. One exchanges with strangers for whom one has no benevolent feelings. Market actors, indeed, typically lose all interest in those with whom they have exchanged; the social relationship established through exchange commonly begins and ends at the point of sale. What people do with the bread sold to them is their business. If that bread remains uneaten and they starve, so be it.

Similarly, in their productive activities prior to market exchange, producers of marketable goods (at least before the post-Fordist techniques that permit direct consumer solicitation of production) were often not directly attentive to other exchange-market participants. Productive activities were clearly influenced by the hope, possibly bolstered by market research, that people will want to buy the goods brought to market one day. But companies could, in principle, proceed in productive activities apart from any direct engagement with participants in those future commercial exchanges. In contrast to a planned economy, companies have not, for example, decided to produce what others out of need actively solicited from them. Actual engagement with others awaits market exchange itself; the activities of producers become social, in short, only in and through that exchange market.[25]

The hand of finance-dominated markets, as we have seen, is not so invisible, since the mechanisms for market coordination so often involve person-to-person, intentional forms of competitive rivalry. What is good for oneself is not thereby usually good for others. Unlike simple commercial markets for exchange (of the sort Adam Smith talked about), it is not just that one does not intend the good of others; what one does out of self-interest is not in fact good for them when markets are organized by direct personal rivalry.

Moreover, the coordination that does remain behind the backs of market participants often ends up being, in contrast to the invisible hand of ordinary commercial markets, not for the good of all either. There are plenty of unintended consequences in labor markets organized by the effort to best others, for example. I am trying to establish my personal value by being better than everyone else, and everyone else is trying to do that too. What ends up happening, however, is what nobody wants: near universal defeat in the effort.

Rather than being mutually beneficial, the actions of each participant in these markets become a form of self-sabotage. It is in principle impossible, for instance, to permanently secure one's personal value to one's employer through efforts to best others. The effect of such efforts can never be finalized or completed; one never ends up simply having a personal value, as a kind of achieved state to be counted on. Because of the purely positional character of the goods being sought, the race is never over. And there is always another race to run—a new employer deadline for some new job demanding different skills.[26] The self-defeating dynamics here are similar to those found in status-oriented consumer markets. One establishes the value of one's person by distinguishing oneself by purchasing what others have not got, but one's success is at best momentary and vanishes as soon as others follow suit. Then the process starts again. The invested energy is wasted, and nobody wins.[27]

For all the insistence on assuming individual responsibility for one's fortunes in finance-dominated capitalism, profiting oneself does depend on the cooperation of others. One needs others to do what serves one's own interests. And this sets up very peculiar dynamics. Others have to do what one wants them to, if profits are to be generated at all, but at the same time one needs to keep others from those profits and reserve them for oneself as much as possible—and that means establishing a kind of independence from them.

Commercial and labor markets always presuppose that participants in them are not economically self-sufficient. If people could support themselves on the basis of what they already own, they would not have to work for others. If producers could themselves make quantities of product sufficient to turn a profit on their investment in equipment, they would not need to hire anyone else to work for them. If people could provide for themselves everything they needed and wanted, they would have no particular reason to enter exchange markets. People bring products to market in order to gain from others what they do not produce for themselves, in exchanges that money broadens quite considerably. Whatever one produces, so long as one has money, one can buy whatever one might conceivably ever need; what one offers in exchange—money— will always be accepted.

To a great extent finance-dominated capitalism simply intensifies this kind of dependence on the cooperation of others if one is to profit oneself. Making a sufficient rate of return within finance-dominated corporations requires, as we have seen, not just getting people to work for a company but getting them to desire what their employer desires. It is not enough for employees to cooperate in the pursuit of ends not their own; their own interests have to converge with those of their employer for the latter to get the most out of their employees.

Certainly within markets for financial assets in particular, profiting oneself depends in an unusually intense way on the actions of others. If they buy as an investment what one has already bought, then one profits. If they decline to buy, those profits suffer. Buying the stock of a good company is not sufficient; other people need to do what one is also doing—just, ideally, not ahead of one.

For good reason, therefore, independent thinking is often overwhelmed by commonly held opinion in financial markets. Since following the herd is the way to profit in markets that move in tandem with market opinion, one's own view of the value of a stock does not matter (at least in the short term) unless other people share it. Market participants are often willing to act, then, against their own better judgment and tend to discount their personal opinions when they differ from those of the majority of market participants. And because everyone else is thinking the same thing about the buying behavior of everyone else, path-dependent information cascades easily arise.

Once a critical mass of people, for reasons no one really understands, gets the ball rolling in purchasing stock, the trend tends to continue unabated. A consensus about market opinion can in this way solidify even when the majority of market participants think that nothing lies behind it, that is, when each of them believes common opinion about stock values to be false.[28]

No market participant in such a buying spree has an interest in ending the party early by expressing strong reservations about whether current stock prices are justified by fundamentals or just absurdly overinflated. Besides ending the rally prematurely, sounding the alarm might encourage others to cash out before one has a chance to, thereby lowering one's own returns when one sells. It is thus preferable to keep quiet until the best time to act, at the top of the market, before the inevitable burst in the bubble that brings market collapse. Or sound the alarm only after one has already sold—or taken steps to short the market.

This exaggerated dependence of profit-making on others in finance-dominated capitalism is matched by an exaggerated need to secure profits for oneself in the most advantageous way. Finance-dominated capitalism, as we have seen, sets the bar at a very high rate of profit across the whole economic spectrum. It is not enough to pay workers a little less than the value they contribute to the product—try instead to pay them much less.

Nonetheless, dependence on others is to one's advantage in finance-dominated capitalism only if some independence from others can be maintained. Employers gain the upper hand, for example, just to the extent they do not depend on specific workers. If current employees demand a greater share of company profits, or just prove insufficiently dedicated to company ends, fire and replace them with more docile and committed ones.

The dependence of workers and employers is somewhat mutual. An employer does not profit to the high degree demanded by finance capitalism without highly cooperative workers whose various activities are coordinated to be maximally productive. And workers do not profit unless the company does so as well, since their pay (no matter how unjustly low) comes out of corporate profits. But employers remain to a significant degree more independent of their workers than workers can ever be independent of their employers. In finance-disciplined corporations, workers have to conform their desires perfectly to those of employers, while employers do not have to pay any attention to worker complaints where they diverge from company objectives. In a labor market in which companies can hire and fire at will, as the value of their stock dictates, employers can simply ignore worker opinions.[29]

One can also establish a very profitable independence from others in financial markets by eventually going one's own way and selling, after a run up in prices, before others do. Like the worker liquidity that gives employers the upper hand—their ability to replace workers at will—the liquidity of secondary markets provides the requisite independence here: the ability to sell investments at any time (assuming the market has not already been spooked).

Rather than taking steps to establish actual independence from others, one can, moreover, simply refuse to recognize it and profit that way. Finance-dominated capitalism, as we have seen, foists individual responsibility on capitalism's losers, but this also allows for moralist self-congratulation among winners. Although one in fact depends on others, one claims all the credit rather than acknowledge that dependence; in so doing, one maximizes one's profit over and against those others. One convinces the boss, say, that one was responsible for all the really important contributions that led to a team's success; for that reason one's remuneration goes way up while that of the other team members takes a hit. One may very well believe one merited the increase since the whole work environment encourages one to think one is being paid what one deserves.

The attribution of responsibility for failure—allowing individuals to be blamed—is here matched by similarly individually oriented praise. And at the root of both praise and blame lies one's individual work ethic, which determines whether one deserves either success or failure.

Every benefit apparently received from others now becomes a function of work—even welfare benefits earned through the responsible search for employment. Similarly, the ability to prudently protect one's assets is a product of work; purchasing private insurance, for example, typically requires paid employment.

Success is one's own achievement for which one takes sole credit. One's value is produced by one's own hard work. In succeeding, one has made the most of what one was given, doing everything required to increase the value of the asset that is one's own person. One is therefore self-made in a quite literal sense: not by amassing external goods or by surrounding oneself with the external trappings of success, but by turning oneself into a profit-generating asset.

Hard work is made the reason for success, with an insistence every bit as strong as anything found in the old Protestant work ethic, and yet the profit-generating mechanisms of finance-dominated capitalism give little reason to valorize hard work. The most lucrative forms of employment in finance-dominated capitalism are, for example, scalable, with the money made in them not increasing in line with the hours worked or energy expended.[30] Reward in such jobs is simply not commensurate with time and effort, between which no direct causal connection exists.

Those making the most money in finance-dominated capitalism may be working all the time with incredible intensity, but commonly there is only an incidental connection between that effort and those profits. For example, a financial trader may spend all his time glued to a computer screen, looking for that perfect arbitrage opportunity, but a billion dollars can be made in a nanosecond at the touch of a button, following a signal from a computer program beyond the trader's comprehension. Nothing could be easier—or more profitable.

In financial markets, financial profits are often turned not through effort but as a function of the enormous money at one's disposal. By making huge bets, one moves the market in one's favor. The price of an asset goes up just because of how much one has purchased of it.

People in jobs where monetary reward is not scalable—for example, janitors, dentists, or food-service providers where hours worked and degree of effort determine earnings)—typically do not make much money at all compared to top earners. The earnings gap within finance-dominated capitalism—between the top and everyone else—is notoriously large. That rewards are commensurate with hard work is not the experience of those who work in nonscalable jobs. Only the people with scalable jobs, in which profit cannot be directly correlated with time and effort, reap the big bucks.

Several other features of finance-dominated capitalism also conflict with the supposition of merited reward. It is hard, therefore, to see the merit where success depends on luck in market timing. The amount of money in retirement accounts may differ according to how hard one has worked, but if one happens to retire when the market is at its peak, one retires rich;

if one retires in a trough, one retires poor. The number of successful investment fund managers is the number one would predict if success were simply a matter of luck.[31]

Acknowledgment of luck does not prevent people from taking credit for it. One finding of the dictator games used by behavioral economists is that people commonly turn luck into a matter of personal merit. What one has obtained entirely by chance—by, say, flipping a coin—is considered as much one's own as anything one had to work hard for; one is therefore similarly reluctant to part with any of it.[32] In keeping with these general findings in behavioral economics, market traders often congratulate themselves for being at the right place at the right time, for being smarter, faster, and cleverer than all those suckers who sold their stock too late.[33]

Winner-take-all markets are another case in point, for it is their very nature to exaggerate the significance of small differences. For example, when performance pay uses relative benchmarks, the few workers who remain may be only very slightly more productive than those let go. Similarly, there may be little difference in price and quality between the goods of one supplier and those of the other suppliers forced into bankruptcy by the former's cornering of the market. Such small differences seem incommensurate with the rewards they bring.

A New Christian World

All I have said in the course of these six chapters suggests that the work ethic of finance-dominated capitalism is incompatible with fundamental Christian commitments. In this last section I spell out the conflict.

First, there is surprisingly little reason to think Christianity has a direct interest in developing a work ethic at all, whatever the form that ethic takes. Certainly prior to the Reformation, Christianity valued specifically religious pursuits, such as contemplative prayer, over work for economic ends, which was viewed with suspicion. If there was a work ethic here, it was exceedingly minimal and highly negative: economic labor was of no particular interest in its own right and was to be avoided whenever it posed a threat to what was of real concern, a life dedicated to God. In stripping one of energy to pursue religious matters and distracting one from that goal, hard work was not a good thing; indeed at its root it was dehumanizing. Someone, of course, had to do the hard work necessary to ensure material well-being, but that work was ordered, in teleological fashion, to higher religious ends. Some people worked in fields and markets to provide others with the leisure to pursue knowledge and love of God full-time.[34]

The Reformation did not so much dispute this ranking as extend it over every sphere of human life, the economic included. Service and worship of God remained of paramount importance, but now anyone could take up those pursuits in and through their everyday activities. The ethic of the monastery, which downplayed economic labor in favor of spiritual pursuits, was not so much repudiated as extended to cover everything. Monastic life itself was to be condemned insofar as it represented a restrictive monopoly on the sort of life that could be dedicated to God.

That devotion to God could be pursued just as well in activities that were not specifically religious in nature elevated the value of those activities, but often not directly. For example, the character of economic activity—its involving hard work, for instance—was not what made it of religious interest; its religious value came from one's ability to express devotion to God in and through such work. The same old religious concerns about work, about its capacity to enervate and misdirect one's energies, could therefore still surface. Given the extraordinary demands placed on workers within finance-dominated capitalism, such concerns are, one would think, only more pertinent now. It is hard to see how the complete exhaustion that comes from spending twenty-four hours a day working could contribute in a positive way to one's religious life.

Indeed, the very fact that economic activity was not considered valuable in its own right was key to what Max Weber thought made certain forms of Protestantism so economically significant. To get up and running, capitalism required people to work hard for its own sake, without any particular concern about enjoying the fruits of their labor. Capitalism, for example, required people to save and continually defer spending on themselves—to exhibit a certain asceticism, in other words—so as to amass capital for investment purposes. But work could become an end in itself in this sense, something to be pursued without regard for its pleasurable consequences, only when people worked for reasons that had nothing to do with their own material enjoyment—for example to satisfy a religious interest in knowing whether they were saved or not. Capitalism was thereby furthered by people who were, in effect, willing to sacrifice their economic interests in material well-being to religious interests.

Of course this devaluation of economic activity per se is mitigated when that activity itself becomes a way of serving God. Especially in some forms of Lutheranism, one can serve God directly in economic pursuits because those are thought to be themselves divine vocations, part of God's specific plans for one's life. Working very hard would amount, then, to an appropriately heightened form of service to God, a way of proving dedication to the God who assigns people to just those tasks.

Such direct attribution of religious value to economic activity importantly complicates any sharp disjunction between religious and this-worldly ends. Rather than deferring enjoyment of salvation until after death, working out one's salvation in Christ would also mean working now for one's own material well-being and that of the world. Salvation would not simply await the resurrection of bodies to come but would be operative now to transform material lives for the better. The gift of Christ that enables personal transformation would be at work throughout the whole of life so as to transform economic activities for the better too.

The problem with direct assignment of religious value to economic pursuits is that it provides religious sanction for whatever form of employment society happens to saddle one with, no matter how limiting or degrading. What is established is assumed proper because part of God's providential arrangement of the world. If, however, salvation includes the material well-being of bodies, and the Christ who brings about that salvation is at work now to transform lives, this sort of sanctification of established forms of economic injustice makes little sense, I believe. If it is possible to serve God in the exhausting and demeaning work one is currently assigned, how much the better might one serve God in forms of employment more in keeping with God's own efforts to bring about the well-being of all? The world's current economic organization would have to be changed to further God's universally beneficent intentions. Christ in enabling our radical self-reformation is presumably giving us the power to make changes in our economic lives too.

Religious ends still take priority here over simply economic ones. For that reason, as we saw in chapter 3, religious priorities always sit somewhat loosely with economic commitments, which they relativize and into which they will not be absorbed. But these effects are a function of the way religious commitments include economic ones within a project to transform life as a whole; a changed way of pursuing economic well-being is a positive part of that religious project.

While I have described it in terms redolent of the enterprise self of contemporary capitalism, this Protestant project conforms no more to capitalism's work ethic than it does to capitalism's sense of enterprise. Indeed, the peculiar way this religious project is an enterprise, so as to form a project fundamentally at odds with that of a contemporary enterprise self, is reproduced here. The ethic of this religious project is just as odd, so odd, indeed, as to amount to a kind of anti-work ethic.

Fundamentally, success in such a religious project is not one's own doing and therefore cannot be an ordinary enterprise. One enters such a project with some realistic hope of success as a result of Christ's influence. One cannot argue or will oneself into such a project apart from Christ's influence. The total commitment that defines such a project cannot be assured simply by one's making greater efforts. Christ is the motor that initiates and propels such a project. One cannot therefore take credit for its success.

One is called to work out one's salvation in leading a different sort of life, but leading that life remains Christ's gift. Self-reformation is achieved only by way of Christ's own working in and through one's own activity. Any contribution that is simply one's own apart from Christ impedes such progress. Working independently of Christ, so as to claim for oneself the responsibility for success, leaves one alone with one's sin.

Because Christ brings it about, conformity to God's will, success in one's calling, cannot simply be one's own individual responsibility. While such conformity does require one's own efforts, success is not contingent on them. Profitable employment in a religious project is not in one's own hands at the most basic of levels. Success is a function of divine power; one therefore has nothing to fear from even the bleakest moments of one's own sinful incapacity and failure.

For these reasons, success in a religious project does nothing to establish individual worth over and against others. Indeed, to the extent one can claim simple personal responsibility for it, such success never amounts to much. Compared to the sinless standard of Christ's own life, the significance of differences of achievement among graced sinners is reduced to nothing: all in whom sin remains fall radically short. Indeed, a life fully dedicated to God, as was Christ's, is an all-or-nothing affair; one is either defined by such a way of life by virtue of one's relation to Christ or one is not. As a qualitatively distinct form of life enabled by Christ's life within one, that life is fundamentally not of a kind to be approximated by degrees or approached incrementally. The degree of success that marks our own achievement concerns only the degree to which our lives manage to exhibit such a qualitative change of state, which is Christ's doing and not our own. And even were one successfully to display the form of a new life in Christ across the whole of one's life in every respect, one is still not permitted to distinguish oneself in any fundamental way from others. They are capable of the same thing one is—and with Christ's help will one day achieve it too—by virtue of what one shares with them.

Gone thereby is any point in trying to gain comparative advantage over others by besting them in the pursuit of religious ends. One's individual worth as someone graced by Christ is not fundamentally dependent on how one stands relative to others. The wider world's search for distinction in competitive contests is thoroughly repudiated; no new, specifically religious form of such contests exists. The standard against which one measures one's person here—Christ's own way of being—is absolute rather than relative. The means of meeting that standard are available to all in the form of Christ himself, rather than being conditional on individual effort. And the state that marks that success can be shared by all without distinction. My gaining salvation does not exclude any one else from it. Salvation is not a scarce good to be fought over. Nor is it accessed through partition in ways that suggest others' enjoyment of it might take away from mine. Christians hope one day to bask all together in the fullness of the very same good that is God's glory. Indeed, the more I think salvation a private property secured by excluding others from it the more I have reason to worry about my ever attaining it. The more God has turned it into a kind of exclusive possession for some, by, say, setting conditions on eligibility, the more I have reason to worry too.[35]

What matters in the end is one's relation with God, one's value in God's eyes and not one's relative worth measured against others. Beyond all the jostling for position that leads to profit within finance-disciplined capitalism lies a God whose own value does not go up and down, and who may thereby provide a stable source of one's value. Irrespective of how I may be positioned in relation to others, God remains my creator who has deemed me good and considers me worthy of consideration, however far I may have fallen away from God's intentions. Valuations based on relative position are certainly never severable here, as they are in financial markets, from the external underlying asset—God. However far people may sinfully stray in their relations with one another, they never float free in purely self-contained, purely self-referential fashion apart from that one, God, in and through whom they ultimately find their value.

The follow-the-leader effects of everyone's competitive attempts to keep up with the profits of others in finance-dominated capitalism is short-circuited here by the contrarian possibilities of a standard of value independent of one's position in relation to other human beings. No profit is to be gained from simply matching the behaviors of others by following their opinions about what is a good bet. Nor is one impelled to try to secure one's worth in the eyes of others, by proving one's relative value to one's employer over against others. Losing one's good reputation in the eyes of one's employer, or even one's job, because one failed to meet the ever-changing standard of hard work set by coworkers does not make one a bad person. Working harder to distinguish oneself from others does not make one a better person; indeed, just that sort of competitive contest is excluded in both the new heaven and the new earth.

It also makes little sense to assume individual responsibility for success or failure given the way that this religious project does not single one out as an isolated individual but as a member of a pool. For all one's differences from others, evident in the distinctive way one pursues such a calling, one remains a creature just like them, a sinner just like them, an object of God's redemptive concern just like them. One's differences from others can neither overshadow nor pull one free of those shared conditions. Thereby efforts to exempt oneself from a common condition or fate (from, say, the imploding financial bubble), by taking actions alone (by, say, getting out before everyone else so as to maximize one's own profits), are discouraged.

Christian beliefs about a shared origin and fate entail, in sum, a refusal of the privatizing of risk and reward at the heart of finance-dominated capitalism. One fails, morally and otherwise, in the company of others. And one gains salvation by God's grace alone.

If Christianity encourages one to think of oneself as part of a pool, it nevertheless does not do so at the expense of one's individuality. In creating and redeeming one in Christ, God sees one not simply from within a general perspective encompassing the whole but as the particular person one is. One's specific character as a person, which sets one apart from others, is the object of God's concern insofar as God creates, guides, and redeems from sin.

Running directly contrary to a work ethic, however, one's value in God's eyes is not *conditional* upon particular achievements that distinguish one from others. One remains of value in God's eyes even if one fails completely (as everyone in some fundamental sense does) in the effort to do what God asks. God remains one's savior even and especially as a sinner. Individuals do set themselves off from others through the particular achievements that help to establish their distinctive individuality. Since God loves them as the particular persons they are, God will love that about them too (at least to the extent their individuality does not simply amount to a sinful grasping of distinction from others). But those achievements are not the fundamental reason they are the valued subjects of God's concern; that concern precedes those achievements and does not vary with them. God does not love you more when you succeed than when you fail, if greater love means demonstrating increased concern for your well-being.

It is not simply that God's love precedes its object in unconditional fashion; God also does not create and save people for the sake of some objective they are tasked with pursuing. God's purpose in creating and saving them is not for them to engage in some sort of productive activity; a work ethic could therefore have no part in that purpose.

God does not create and save people because God needs something from them, something that requires hard work from them. God does not act out of need, in order to gain something God lacks apart from our efforts. God does want people to live lives in complete dedication to God's will, but that is not why God creates or saves them to begin with. God simply wants to share God's life, so that the fullness of that life is reflected in something not God. Indeed, in creating and saving us, God is doing all that is necessary to communicate that fullness of God's life to us, over and against the impediments posed by our sins, which ultimately require God's coming into the world in Christ. Given that we are created to know and to will, God intends that we reflect God's life in and through our own active and deliberate efforts to dedicate our lives to God.[36]

While we are created by God to be productive of our lives in this way—to make ourselves over with God's help into God's image—we are not necessarily called in any other respect to be productive, that is, to produce anything else. There is no reason to think, as the anthropology of production typical of capitalism (and its Marxist critique) does, that we can produce ourselves only by producing other things. Some sort of work on things is needed to generate the material well-being that is part of our imaging of God's life of supreme well-being. But Christians associate hard work and especially hard labor with the fall; there was no need for extreme effort in Eden before the disordering of the world as God intended it.

Capitalism may enhance (in principle at least) the ability of humans to be productive of their own material well-being; lots of things that (some) people currently enjoy are inconceivable apart from the coordination of activity in machine-enabled production. But the inclusion of material well-being in the human imaging of God's well-being does not necessitate this particular mechanism for life-enhancement, with its demands for intense, effort-filled work.

Moreover, according to this understanding of God's rela-tions with the world, value does not enter the world through us, by virtue of mixing our labor with it. The materials upon which we work have value prior to our activity insofar as they form the non-purposive "products" of God's creative activity. God created them for no purpose or end other than to be the reflections of God's glory. We are similarly not responsible for creating the value of what we are and will be through produc-tive activities, whether on ourselves or other things. The fun-damentally non-purposive, and in that sense non-productive, activity of God should underlie all our productive activity, as-suring its fundamental value, whatever our particular capacities and their measure of success.

With an anthropology of production in which human work is the source of value fundamentally undermined, the heightened work ethic of finance-dominated capitalism col-lapses. One can no longer expect personal fulfillment through work in any ordinary sense of that.

If the work ethic of contemporary capitalism is to be overthrown, it is no longer sufficient to eradicate work's alien-ating qualities by making work enjoyable, as contemporary capitalism promises—in fact, demands. Take pleasure in the work itself, it insists, irrespective of its product (which remains in company hands); consider work a valuable form of self-expression, a means to self-realization. The more one expects from work, the more comprehensive and complete its supposed generation of value, the less likely it is to fulfill that expectation.[37]

Nor is it enough to extend productive activities beyond gainful employment, carving out time and energy for what one would rather do.[38] One might cut back on work—assuming one is still paid enough to avoid starvation—to make room for production of a more homespun, less capital-intensive sort, like craftwork and bread-baking.[39] Or one might find time and space for oneself outside the time and space colonized by paid employment—maybe in bed between three and four o'clock in the morning?—so as to experiment on working on oneself for ends established solely by oneself and one's freely chosen companions.[40] Even if feasible, by seeking freedom in work all such tactics presuppose work's value, its value-producing capacities.

Or to resist one might inhabit arenas of life that capitalism, with its insistence on productivity, expels. One could defiantly make the most of forced unemployment, wearing one's lack of productivity as a badge of honor by lazing about in unproductive pursuits and, where necessary to support oneself, taking out loans one never intends to pay back.[41] Even more defiantly, one could call a general strike, refusing to work and burning the notes for the loans that need forced one to assume.[42] Or more defiantly still, one might revel in what is positively unproductive by purposely engaging in destructive behavior that wastes assets.[43]

Unfortunately for this sort of strategy, exclusion from gainful employment has become a primary way of making money in finance-dominated capitalism—that is indeed what forces people into debt, where the real money is to be made. And failure is the very thing that the instruments of money-making in finance-dominated capitalism lead one to expect. That expectation is the reason, for example, why nonperforming loans have so commonly been fobbed onto someone else before becoming worthless. Failure anticipated is turned into a source of profit. It is why bonds created by bundling loans can have such a high interest rate. In general, one cannot overthrow what one leaves in place by vacating the field. Or, in case of a universal debt and work strike, one is left with a simple negative: if no work and no debt, then what?

What is to replace such acts of resistance, along the Christian lines developed here, is a community forged according to very different assumptions about how relations to oneself bear on relations with others. This anti-work ethic has its own social presuppositions and implications, with the capacity to form a whole alternative world.

Recognition of dependence on God is what informs this Foucault-styled ethic, which is dissociated from the need for hard work. Recognition of dependence on God shapes how one relates to oneself as the moral subject of action.[44] Because one depends on God rather than on oneself in this most fundamental of relations with oneself, one should be willing to recognize dependence on other people too. The profit-making mechanisms in finance-dominated capitalism that refuse to acknowledge such dependence would thus be countered.

The religious project is a cooperative project; other people are in it with you and therefore can help you by, for instance, supplying examples of what engagement in that project looks like (for better or worse). That the religious project is a cooperative project is in keeping with God's own objectives for the world: God in Christ is effecting a divine kingdom, a community with a divine foundation under divine direction.

But more than this, one's dependence on God requires some degree of dependence on others for its communication to oneself as a life project. The recognition of dependence on God that undergirds such a project always takes its start from others already so committed to living in conformity with what God has done for them in Christ. Whether anyone knows it or not, God is indeed working to transform the character of human life, and in that sense independently of the deliberate life projects of other human beings. The world is different because of Christ even if no one recognizes that fact and attempts to live accordingly. But one can knowingly and willingly make what Christ achieves alone the basis of one's life project now only by depending on other witnesses to its meaning for their lives.

Christ's human life is the primary witness to what God's being one with the human should mean for human life. Upon his death, the witness of others to Christ himself—their attempt to lead the sort of life he did—extends this effort of attestation over time, albeit imperfectly. Indeed, although only God empowers the human transformations that mark saved existence, God never enters anyone's life to transform it without the mediation of that power that starts with Christ's humanity and that extends its own influence through the incorporation of other humans as members of his body. Christ's influence remains irreplaceable, but upon his death his very own influence is conveyed through other human beings who form a community of life with him, in a very literal sense: humans who are dead to themselves in that they now live his very life, their own lives being fundamentally remade insofar as they become an extension of his. Humans who are already in the process of being remade in him, witnessing to him, orienting their lives by him, convey to others this same community of life with Christ in his physical absence.[45]

Dependence on God does not collapse, however, into dependence on others. One is therefore not encouraged to submerge oneself within the community of others for the sake of one's own profit in the way finance-dominated capitalism encourages an extremely intense dependence on others. Everyone else, aside from Christ himself, fundamentally fails in the religious project that Christ empowers: everyone else continues to some degree to struggle against sin. To the extent that people influence others by virtue of their own persons, rather than by

virtue of Christ's own influence within them, they tend to impede the religious project of others—because of the sin that
remains in the way they show forth Christ's influence on them.
Indeed, even were they to conquer sin entirely and manifest
Christ with complete transparency, they would hamper the
religious project of others just to the extent their own personal influence became the focus and replaced that of Christ.
They would become the motor for the transformation of others in a kind of sinful substitution for Christ. Ironically, one
cannot imagine a more corrupting influence than such a self-
referential form of religious communication, yet on the part of
persons who otherwise appear to be saints. For the same reason
a focus on the saintliness of the human communicators of
Christ's influence—say, in ways that encourage a refusal of
communion with religious leaders who appear more sinful than
others (as in the Donatist controversy)—is similarly corrupting
for a communally fostered religious project.

One should never be dependent on others in the way one
is on God. Doing so would turn those others into idols with a
self-defeating, destructive effect on one's own religious project.
While they may be helping one succeed, such people cannot
secure one's profit as God does. They are just as vulnerable to
sin as oneself, and for that reason one must continually work
to shore them up if they are to pretend to perform the work
that only God can do. One is thereby enslaved to such idols,
forced into constant, unending, and ultimately futile work for
the benefit of the very supposedly saintly persons that one
counted on to insure one's own profit.[46]

Once initiated into that conscious community of life with
Christ with the help of others, one can go it alone if necessary,
without, that is, any further intentional help. One can, in other
words, make progress in one's religious project while sur-

rounded by sinners who influence one in highly distorted ways—by, for example, drawing attention to their own saintliness in self-congratulatory fashion. That progress is at root empowered by Christ and not by them.

The Christian religious project thus does not stand out from that of the enterprise self of contemporary capitalism simply by being a cooperative project in which each person makes a distinctive contribution. In financial capitalism as in every form of capitalism, value is produced by coordinating activities (through the use of machines) to bring about what no one person could. They may not be intending to help one another in this joint enterprise, but if what I am saying about Christian community is correct, Christians may not be working very intentionally to help others either. Their good effect on others—for example, their communication of Christ's life to them—is often, instead, an unintended consequence of horribly flawed efforts to lead a Christian life. The ability to continue alone—empowered by fundamental dependence on God rather than on other people—is perhaps where the Christian religious project differs most fundamentally from a current capitalist one.

In the effort to counter the way people are encouraged to seize profit over against others in contemporary capitalism, it is not enough to counsel that everyone should be valued commensurately with their contributions in a cooperative project, as if that were the distinctive contribution of Christianity to an understanding of properly organized sociability.[47] Pay commensurate with individual contributions to team outcomes is the very ideology of contemporary capitalism. What is unusual about Christianity—and what is much harder for contemporary capitalism to fathom—is the idea that efforts retain their value even apart from any obviously and intentionally positive contribution to a project requiring the cooperative coordination of tasks.

The body of Christ is such a cooperative body but its head plays a very peculiar role. All the work of the body is attributed to the head. And once the body as a whole is alive through its head, the failure of members does not prevent that head from retaining the very same enlivening influence on remaining members.

When compared with the social forms of finance-dominated capitalism, this communal body is also unusual in its non-rivalrous form of social coordination. By contrast with the personal rivalry found in finance-dominated markets, rivalry is headed off using mechanisms with certain structural similarities to those of earlier forms of capitalism. Personal rivalries over relative contributions or achievements within the body are prevented because social relations with others are always being mediated through some external third thing—God.

Thus, community members are not directly coordinating their actions with one another to form a community of life based on their own estimations of who is succeeding or failing in such a religious project, in what respect, or by how much. Each member is instead trying, as a particular individual with a specific history, to conform one's life to God's will, and in the process, as a secondary effect, one's respective actions can become coordinated in a mutually supportive way. That is, the more each is successful in such a pursuit the more likely it is that others will be too by way of their influence, with the efforts of one complementing or supplementing those of others, and so on. The God who stands outside those human relations is in this sense entering into those relations to do the coordination of them, behind their backs and independently of their own intentions. Although the conscious project of relationship with

God is communicated via other persons, one is not required to be actively and directly engaged with them in any other respect, as anything more than communicators of Christ's own influence. Indeed, to the extent that others communicate the project of engagement with Christ properly, they turn one away from themselves to God in Christ. In this sense, one is actively related to others socially only through the relationship that one has with God independently of others.

Moreover, although everyone wants what everyone else wants here—to live a life transparent to the life of Christ within one—members do not compete with one another for those same goods because of a certain detachment from those goods that the relationship to that third thing, God, enables. God functions here something like the way money functions: to allow one to give up one's attachments to the achievements that others would also like for themselves. There is no achievement that cannot be replaced. One can always do something else, something different, something more, to display wholehearted commitment to God. If one is genuinely committed to God rather than to the human good God makes possible—say, saintliness—one should be willing to give up that human good—let someone else have the distinction of displaying that saintliness—whenever attachment to it threatens to displace commitment to God.

Finally, the Christian variant of such mechanisms heads off the critique often made of the form such mechanisms take in earlier market society: because social relations go by way of something outside them, the community can exhibit no strong horizontal ties. The critique here would be similar to that leveled against insurance provided by either the welfare state or private means: the relations established with others become almost de-socialized, especially when compared with those comprising mutual-aid societies. In a program of social welfare, for example, people are only really related to the state that is pooling their money for redistribution purposes and that is responsible for directing it to people in need. People thereby lose any direct personal relationships with the other people who are coming to their aid.[48]

But in the Christian case of mediation of social relations by something outside them, one is not simply partaking separately of what one at most may know everyone else is enjoying separately too. Despite its orientation to something outside of one's relations with others, one's own enjoyment is directly fed and magnified by theirs. The experience is something like watching a sunset with someone else. One is very glad to share the experience; other people's presence enhances one's own experience. The external mediation of relations to others here by way of a third thing—the sun—hardly means one is indifferent to those others, isolated in one's own private experience; to the contrary, one cares about them and the character of their own experience. If, for example, something is hindering their enjoyment—for example, they are in pain—it would be better for all concerned to remedy that. A genuine community of enjoyment is being set up here in virtue of the peculiar character of what externally mediates it, something that can best be enjoyed with others, the more of them the better.

This sort of expansiveness remedies the defect of usually tight-knit, personally mediated communities of mutual support: they tend to be quite small and have rather strict conditions for membership. For example, mutual insurance societies typically limit membership to physically fit, gainfully employed hard workers. It is counterproductive to fill the ranks of such a society with sick loafers, for that would guarantee that the society would run out of money paying claims and go belly up.[49]

There is no point indeed in aiming at the sort of good that discourages rivalry if one only ever enjoys it alone. Enjoying it alone hides its character. Insisting on lonely enjoyment distorts that good's character; it shows one fundamentally misunderstands it.

The character of God, which establishes the proper manner in which one relates to God, makes all the difference here, as Augustine well knew. Thus, if one were related to God as a part to a whole, because, as in Manichaeism, divinity was itself like something extended in space—subject to partition and found in greater or lesser quantities depending on whether circumstances were hostile—then, yes, possession would amount to the always potentially conflict-ridden matter of who can amass the most of it. One would gain more of God by literally having more of God. Because of its spatially extended nature, evil forces of darkness are able to hem divinity in, to break it up to varying degrees by mixing with it, surrounding it with a kind of foreign accretion, and thereby weakening it. Those divided parts or sparks of divinity must be collected together for the salvation of any one of them to be accomplished; the salvation of any one comes about, in other words, by way of communion with the others. And that cooperative communal process proceeds by way of differences of degree of divinity within it. Thus, the elect who have amassed a greater amount of divinity, who are already light-filled, have the direct responsibility for collecting divinity back together again by way of the auditors, of lesser divinity, who literally serve them. The latter are responsible for working for and feeding the former. When divinity is finally collected, relative differences among community members are overcome: each enjoys what all do in an extremely intense form of communion. But this communion is bought at the price of utter homogeneity. As Jason David

BeDuhn has written, "Perfection entails a homogenization of individual selves, an erasure of distinctions, and an opening to direct interpenetration of experience. 'Every thought and reflection obtained and all intentions in mind / Are mutually shown and observed, and no suspicion and misunderstanding exits.' The saved are 'harmonious in mind' and 'every one of them looks the same without exceptional appearance.' 'All natures . . . and forms are equal, and all places bear no differences.' "[50]

On a Christian understanding (influenced by neo-Platonism), the God who is nothing like any of them, and in that sense outside of them all, can be enjoyed as a whole by each and every one of them, through a kind of direct link in each and every case. The very same object of love and knowledge is made the basis of a common vision and desire. The community here is intense. People are united, that is, in ways that overcome all division, but such community is never predicated on the erasure of the individual places from which, in each case, desire and vision begins to end in God. What brings them together to unify them is simply the object upon which they all rest. As the friends assembled by Augustine (and who later joined him as bishop in Hippo) were, Christians are

> united by the vision of a single Beloved, a Supreme Beauty . . . both utterly distant . . . yet hauntingly present. In ceasing to be [like] Manichees they [leave behind] . . . intense horizontal bonding thought of as a blending of like minds. . . . Each one of them [strains] to reach a Beauty whose sheer delight [renders] each one of them forgetful of his or her own self. All [are] drawn together to share in a common . . . joy . . . a shared passion, which [blots] out the normal sense of "mine" and "yours."[51]

Even now, at moments, such experience of God as a whole can be shared in the way Augustine shared it with his mother at Ostia. Ideally, one day (that day that lasts forever) everyone will enjoy such an experience of God together; on that day God will be possessed as a common object of love and knowledge by one and all.

What have I demonstrated, in sum, over the course of this book? I hope I have shown the coherence of a whole new world to be entertained as an imaginative counter to the whole world of capitalism as it presently exists and pretends to be all-encompassing, to have no limits, nothing outside itself. While I hope I have convinced you that it is not at all like the world of finance-dominated capitalism, this new world operates not at a remove from finance-dominated capitalism but by cutting across it, traversing it to disruptive effect, along the very line of the ethics of self-transformation that is the relay or transfer point of its various dimensions, the hinge or axis around which the whole turns, that aspect upon which this entire old world has riveted itself. If I am right such an alternative world requires no resuscitation to resonate with present possibilities for resistance, to be engaged at these nodes of the current system's vulnerability—as Foucault's calling up of ancient Stoicism or Cynicism might suggest the need for resuscitation of a corpse. The power behind this other world has been felt in the past and is still here, no deferred utopia (for simply sublimated expression now) but already at work in the present, with a voice whose force has yet to be extinguished.[52]

Notes

1

The New Spirit of Capitalism and a Christian Reponse

1. Max Weber, *The Protestant Ethic and the Spirit of Capitalism,* trans. Talcott Parsons (New York: Scribner, 1958).

2. R. H. Tawney, foreword, ibid., 1(e); Weber, *Protestant Ethic,* 64.

3. Weber, *Protestant Ethic,* 53.

4. Ibid., 153–154.

5. Ibid., 70.

6. Ibid., 71.

7. See Max Weber, "The Social Psychology of the World Religions," in *From Max Weber: Essays in Sociology,* ed. and trans. H. H. Gerth and C. Wright Mills (New York: Oxford University Press, 1958), 267.

8. Ibid., 280.

9. Weber, *Protestant Ethic,* 97–98.

10. For more on this understanding of the relationship between religious belief and action, see Kathryn Tanner, *Politics of God: Christian Theologies and Social Justice* (Minneapolis: Fortress Press, 1992), chapter 1.

11. Weber, *Protestant Ethic,* 232n66.

12. See Michel Foucault, *The Hermeneutics of the Subject,* trans. Graham Burchell (New York: Picador, 2005), 10–19, and the introduction by Arnold I. Davidson, xxiii–xxvii.

13. This is not to say that capitalism's effects on human conduct are not also machinic (as we shall see in chapter 4), thereby bypassing conscious ideas or representations; it is only to claim that such effects, once reflected upon in cultural (or representational) forms, are what shape the

deliberate conduct of individuals—on the molar level, to use a Deleuzian term. See Maurizio Lazzarato, *Signs and Machines: Capitalism and the Production of Subjectivity,* trans. Joshua David Jordan (Los Angeles: Semiotext[e], 2014).

14. See Pierre Dardot and Christian Laval, *The New Way of the World: On Neoliberal Society,* trans. Gregory Elliott (London: Verso, 2013), 1–18.

15. Weber, *Protestant Ethic,* 47–48.

16. See Luc Boltanski and Eve Chiapello, *The New Spirit of Capitalism,* trans. Gregory Elliott (London: Verso, 2007), 16–19.

17. For this understanding of ideal type, see Max Weber, " 'Objectivity' in Social Science and Social Policy," in his *The Methodology of the Social Sciences,* trans. Edward A. Shils and Henry A. Finch (New York: Free Press, 1949), 49–112. I am constructing an ideal type of finance-dominated capitalism and its spirit on the basis of very extensive reading in contemporary economic theory, only a slight portion of which appears in the notes.

18. Greta R. Krippner, *Capitalizing on Crisis: The Political Origins of the Rise of Finance* (Cambridge: Harvard University Press, 2011), 29.

19. Ibid., chapter 1, offers a critical review of these different explanations. Like the theories Krippner considers insufficient, her own emphasis on political decision-making assumes noncyclical stagnation or permanent low growth as the underlying problem.

20. John Bellamy Foster and Robert W. McChesney, *The Endless Crisis: How Monopoly-Finance Capitalism Produces Stagnation and Upheaval from the USA to China* (New York: Monthly Review, 2012), 60, citing Jan Toporowski, "The Wisdom of Property and the Politics of the Middle-Classes," *Monthly Review* 62, no. 4 (September 2010): 12.

21. John Maynard Keynes, *The General Theory of Employment, Interest and Money* (San Diego: Harvest/Harcourt, 1964), 156.

22. See Edward LiPuma and Benjamin Lee, *Financial Derivatives and the Globalization of Risk* (Durham, NC: Duke University Press, 2004).

23. See Karen Ho, *Liquidated: An Ethnography of Wall Street* (Durham, NC: Duke University Press, 2009), chapters 3–4.

24. See Eileen Appelbaum and Rosemary Blatt, *Private Equity at Work: When Wall Street Manages Main Street* (New York: Russell Sage, 2014).

25. For an extended discussion of the tradeoff between government policies encouraging economic growth and placating financial interests, see Wolfgang Streeck, *Buying Time: The Delayed Crisis of Democratic Capitalism,* trans. Patrick Camiller (London: Verso, 2014).

26. This is the argument in Michel Foucault, *Birth of Biopolitics,* trans. Graham Burchell (New York: Picador, 2008), now extended to finance-dominated capitalism, as has become increasingly common in the second-

ary literature on this work. See, for example, Dardot and Laval, *New Way of the World.*

27. Weber, *Protestant Ethic,* 72.

28. Ibid., 60–61.

29. David Harvey, *Spaces of Hope* (Berkeley: University of California Press, 2000), 237.

30. See Fredric Jameson, *Archaeologies of the Future: The Desire Called Utopia and Other Science Fictions* (London: Verso, 2007), 15.

31. Ibid., 232.

32. See, for example, Foucault, *Hermeneutics of the Subject,* 181, 211.

33. Ibid., 182.

2
Chained to the Past

1. Maurizio Lazzarato, *The Making of Indebted Man: An Essay on the Neoliberal Condition,* trans. Joshua David Jordan (Los Angeles: Semiotext[e], 2012), 112.

2. Ibid., 45, discussing Friedrich Nietzsche. I am extending his analysis of the temporal features of debt to cover changed workplace conditions under finance-dominated capitalism.

3. See, for example, the account of overwork among software engineers in Ofer Sharone, "Engineering Overwork: Bell-Curve Management at a High-Tech Firm," in *Fighting for Time: Shifting Boundaries of Work and Social Life,* ed. Cynthia Fuchs Epstein and Arne L. Kalleberg (New York: Russell Sage, 2004), 193–201, and the description of the way heightened performance demands are combined with self-management among retail workers in Paul du Gay, *Consumption and Identity at Work* (London: Sage, 1996), 129–137, 162–165.

4. See, for example, Jill Andresky Fraser, *White Collar Sweat-Shop: The Deterioration of Work and Its Rewards in Corporate America* (New York: Norton, 2001), 24, 30, 32, 42–43, 175.

5. See Paul Langley, *The Everyday Life of Global Finance: Saving and Borrowing in Anglo-America* (Oxford: Oxford University Press, 2008), 203–204.

6. See, for example, André Orléan, *The Empire of Value: A New Foundation for Economics,* trans. M. B. DeBevoise (Cambridge: MIT Press, 2014), 208–211.

7. Jean-Pierre Durand, *The Invisible Chain: Constraints and Opportunities in the New World of Employment* (New York: Palgrave Macmillan, 2007), 32–34, 46–47, 75–77. See also the description of the "effort-biased" character

of measures to improve the efficiency of production flows in Francis Green, *Demanding Work: The Paradox of Job Quality in the Affluent Economy* (Princeton, NJ: Princeton University Press, 2006), 48–49, 69–72.

8. See David Weil, *The Fissured Workplace: Why Work Became So Bad for So Many and What Can Be Done to Improve It* (Cambridge: Harvard University Press, 2014).

9. See, for example, the analysis of the financial motives behind subprime lending to minority communities in Dan Immergluck, *Foreclosed: High-Risk Lending, Deregulation, and the Undermining of America's Mortgage Market* (Ithaca, NY: Cornell University Press, 2009).

10. See the series of articles by Jessica Silver-Greenberg and Michael Corkery, Driven into Debt, *New York Times,* 2014–2015, available at http://dealbook.nytimes.com/category/series/driven-into-debt/.

11. Susanne Soederberg, *Debtfare States and the Poverty Industry: Money, Discipline and the Surplus Population* (New York: Routledge, 2014), 163.

12. Ibid., 63.

13. See Wolfgang Streeck, *Buying Time: The Delayed Crisis of Democratic Capitalism,* trans. Patrick Camiller (London: Verso, 2014), chapter 2.

14. See Eileen Appelbaum and Rosemary Blatt, *Private Equity at Work: When Wall Street Manages Main Street* (New York: Russell Sage, 2014), chapters 2–3.

15. See Lazzarato, *Making of Indebted Man,* 47, 57–60.

16. See, for example, the description of "job spill" in Fraser, *White Collar Sweat-Shop,* 24–28.

17. Foucault himself, given his particular understanding of capitalism's construction of human subjectivity (discussed in the next chapter), was interested in possibilities opened up by ancient Stoicism and Cynicism for gay life in the present.

18. See Nathan Eubank, *Wages of Cross-Bearing and Debt of Sin: The Economy of Heaven in Matthew's Gospel* (Berlin: De Gruyter, 2013), 163, 166. See also Gary A. Anderson, *Sin: A History* (New Haven: Yale University Press, 2009).

19. See Jason David BeDuhn, *Augustine's Manichaean Dilemma,* vol. 1, *Conversion and Apostasy, 373–388 C.E.* (Philadelphia: University of Pennsylvania Press, 2010), 239, and his *Augustine's Manichaean Dilemma,* vol. 2, *Making a "Catholic Self," 388–401 C.E.* (Philadelphia: University of Pennsylvania Press, 2013), 15–16.

20. See Richard B. Hays, *Reading Backwards: Figural Christology and the Fourfold Gospel Witness* (Waco, TX: Baylor University Press, 2014).

21. Ibid., 41.

22. Ibid., 109.

23. For more on the idea of a character-destroying character, see Roberto Unger, *The Religion of the Future* (Cambridge: Harvard University Press, 2014), 366–368.

24. See Jean-Paul Sartre, *Being and Nothingness*, trans Hazel E. Barnes (New York: Washington Square Press, 1977), 247.

25. Michel Foucault, *On the Government of the Living*, trans. Graham Burchell (New York: Palgrave Macmillan, 2014), 177.

26. Thomas F. Torrance, *The Doctrine of Grace in the Apostolic Fathers* (Eugene, OR: Wipf and Stock, 1996), 94, 129, 131.

27. Ibid., 123, 124. See also 119.

28. G. W. H. Lampe, *Reconciliation in Christ* (London: Longman, Green, 1956), 100.

29. See Anderson, *Sin*. I am playing up, as he does not, the unusual features of debt repayment here.

3
Total Commitment

1. See Francis Green, *Demanding Work: The Paradox of Job Quality in the Affluent Economy* (Princeton, NJ: Princeton University Press, 2006), 69.

2. Ibid., 83. More theoretically sophisticated developments of this point, which inform my treatment of it in this chapter, are to be found in Pierre Dardot and Christian Laval, *The New Way of the World: On Neoliberal Society*, trans. Gregory Elliott (London: Verso, 2013), chapter 9; Jean-Pierre Durand, *The Invisible Chain: Constraints and Opportunities in the New World of Employment* (New York: Palgrave Macmillan, 2007); Nikolas Rose, *Governing the Soul: The Shaping of the Private Self*, 2nd ed. (London: Free Association Books, 1999), chapter 10; and Frédéric Lordon, *Willing Slaves of Capital: Spinoza and Marx on Desire*, trans. Gabriel Ash (London: Verso, 2014).

3. Daniel Bell, *The Cultural Contradictions of Capitalism* (New York: Basic Books, 1976).

4. See Durand, *Invisible Chain*, 33.

5. For this account of the machinic, see Maurizio Lazzarato, *Signs and Machines: Capitalism and the Production of Subjectivity*, trans. Joshua David Jordan (Los Angeles: Semiotext[e], 2104).

6. See, for example, Stephen Greenhouse, *The Big Squeeze: Tough Times for the American Worker* (New York: Anchor, 2008), 107–116.

7. See Caitlin Zaloom, "The Discipline of Speculators," in *Global Assemblages: Technology, Politics, and Ethics as Anthropological Problems,* ed. Aihwa Ong and Stephen J. Collier (Oxford: Blackwell, 2005), 253–269.

8. See Lordon, *Willing Slaves,* 32–39.

9. See Paul du Gay, *Consumption and Identity at Work* (London: Sage, 1996), 65.

10. Ibid., 192.

11. See Luc Boltanski and Eve Chiapello, *The New Spirit of Capitalism,* trans. Gregory Elliott (London: Verso, 2007), 486–487.

12. See Michel Foucault, *The Birth of Biopolitics,* trans. Graham Burchell (New York: Picador, 2008), 225–226.

13. See Karen Ho, *Liquidated: An Ethnography of Wall Street* (Durham, NC: Duke University Press, 2009), 172–173.

14. See Dardot and Laval, *New Way of the World,* chapter 8. See also du Gay, *Consumption and Identity,* 186–190.

15. See, for example, Marilyn Strathern, ed., *Audit Cultures: Anthropological Studies in Accountability, Ethics and the Academy* (London: Routledge, 2000).

16. Lordon, *Willing Slaves,* 38.

17. Durand, *Invisible Chain,* 63.

18. For more on this sort of impression management, see David L. Collinson and Margaret Collinson, "The Power of Time: Leadership, Management and Gender," in *Fighting for Time: Shifting Boundaries of Work and Social Life,* ed. Cynthia Fuchs Epstein and Arne L. Kalleberg (New York: Russell Sage, 2004), 231.

19. Lordon, *Willing Slaves,* 83.

20. Ibid., 82.

21. Ibid.

22. Ibid., 145–146.

23. Ibid., 99.

24. See Ho, *Liquidated,* 242, 292, and Zaloom, "Discipline of Speculators," 254.

25. Durand, *Invisible Chain,* 43–44.

26. Lordon, *Willing Slaves,* 101.

27. I have been influenced here by a similar formulation of religious commitment in Noreen Khawaja, *The Religion of Existence: Asceticism in Philosophy from Kierkegaard to Sartre* (Chicago: University of Chicago Press, 2016).

28. This is the distinguishing mark of Christianity as a religion for Friedrich Schleiermacher. See his *On Religion: Speeches to Its Cultured Despisers,* trans. Richard Crouter (Cambridge: Cambridge University Press, 1988), 117–118 (speech 5).

29. See Pierre Hadot, *Exercices spirituels et philosophie antique* (Paris: Albin Michel, 2002), 77, 224, 226.

30. See Éric Rebillard, *Christians and Their Many Identities in Late Antiquity, North Africa, 200–450 CE* (Ithaca, NY: Cornell University Press, 2012), 4.

31. I am opposing here the way both Hadot and Foucault make obedience a distinguishing characteristic of a specifically Christian way of life. See Hadot, *Exercices spirituels,* 97. See, among many other examples, Michel Foucault, *Wrong-Doing, Truth-Telling: The Function of Avowal in Justice,* trans. Stephen W. Sawyer (Chicago: University of Chicago Press, 2014), 138–139, 165.

32. See Kathryn Tanner, *Christ the Key* (Cambridge: Cambridge University Press, 2010), chapter 1.

33. See Elena Esposito, *The Future of Futures: The Time of Money in Financing and Society* (Cheltenham, UK: Edward Elgar, 2011), 52, 54.

34. See Pierre Hadot, *Philosophy as a Way of Life,* trans. Michael Chase (Oxford: Blackwell, 1995), chapters 3, 7.

35. See Dardot and Laval, *New Way of the World,* 273.

36. Hadot, *Philosophy as a Way of Life,* 208.

37. See Michel Foucault, *Security, Territory, Population,* trans. Graham Burchell (New York: Palgrave Macmillan, 2007), 194–202.

38. Ibid., 231 (omitted passage from his original manuscript).

39. See Michel Foucault, *On the Government of the Living,* trans. Graham Burchell (New York: Palgrave Macmillan, 2014), 177–178, and Foucault, *Security, Territory, Population,* 191–216.

4
Nothing but the Present

1. My treatment of scarcity in this chapter follows closely Sendhil Mullainathan and Eldar Shafir, *Scarcity: Why Having Too Little Means So Much* (New York: Henry Holt, 2013). As behavioral economists, the authors are primarily concerned with poverty; while they do consider a broad range of cases of time and resource scarcity and do give some attention to workplace pressures, the extension of their analysis to the management practices of finance-disciplined corporations is my own.

2. Ibid., 69–70.

3. Ibid., especially chapter 2.

4. Ibid., 157.

5. Ibid., chapter 5.

6. Ibid., chapter 6.

7. Ibid., chapter 4.

8. Ibid., chapter 6.

9. See Fredric Jameson, *Postmodernism or the Cultural Logic of Late Capitalism* (Durham, NC: Duke University Press, 1984), 26–28, and the discussion of Jameson in David Harvey, *The Condition of Postmodernity* (Oxford: Blackwell, 1989), 53–54.

10. See Caitlin Zaloom, "The Discipline of Speculators," in *Global Assemblages: Technology, Politics, and Ethics as Anthropological Problems,* ed. Aihwa Ong and Stephen J. Collier (Oxford: Blackwell, 2005), 258–259, 262, 264.

11. Ibid., 260.

12. Ibid., 259.

13. Jameson, *Postmodernism,* 28; Harvey, *Condition of Postmodernity,* 54.

14. Jameson, *Postmodernism,* 27.

15. Harvey, *Condition of Postmodernity,* 53.

16. For this concept of temporal depth, see Allen C. Bluedorn and Stephen P. Harris, "Temporal Depth, Age, and Organizational Performance," in *Fighting for Time: Shifting Boundaries of Work and Social Life,* ed. Cynthia Fuchs Epstein and Arne L. Kalleberg (New York: Russell Sage, 2004), 115–116.

17. Ibid., 121–122.

18. Zaloom, "Discipline of Speculators," 261.

19. Horace quoted in Pierre Hadot, *Philosophy as a Way of Life,* trans. Michael Chase (Oxford: Blackwell, 1995), 88. I am in dialogue with Hadot's treatment of Epicureanism and Stoicism in what follows.

20. Karen Ho, *Liquidated: An Ethnography of Wall Street* (Durham, NC: Duke University Press, 2009), 233.

21. Hadot, *Philosophy as a Way of Life,* 209.

22. See Ho, *Liquidated,* 275–285.

23. Here and in the next couple of paragraphs I follow the analysis of derivatives provided by Edward LiPuma and Benjamin Lee, *Financial Derivatives and the Globalization of Risk* (Durham, NC: Duke University Press, 2004), 37, 116–117, 124, 127–129.

24. See Harvey, *Condition of Postmodernity,* 229–230.

25. See Jean-Pierre Durand, *The Invisible Chain: Constraints and Opportunities in the New World of Employment* (New York: Palgrave Macmillan, 2007), 77–80.

26. See Harvey, *Condition of Postmodernity,* 265.

27. See Bluedorn and Harris, "Temporal Depth," 117.

28. Hadot, *Philosophy as a Way of Life,* 227.

29. See Scott Lash and John Urry, *Economies of Signs and Space* (London: Sage, 1994), 242.

30. Zaloom, "Discipline of Speculators," 261.

31. Ho, *Liquidated,* 275.

32. Ibid., 279.

33. See Mullainathan and Shafir, *Scarcity,* 115–116.

34. One need not therefore make commitment to cultural norms the explanation for continued company attachment to an ultimately unprofitable shareholder-value management style, as Karen Ho does.

35. I am following here the general theory of exploitation by way of relative immobility in Luc Boltanski and Eve Chiapello, *The New Spirit of Capitalism,* trans. Gregory Elliott (London: Verso, 2007), 360–372.

36. Mullainathan and Shafir, *Scarcity,* 150.

37. Miranda Joseph, *Debt to Society: Accounting for Life under Capitalism* (Minneapolis: University of Minnesota Press, 2014), 76.

38. See Jacob S. Hacker, *The Great Risk Shift: The New Economic Insecurity and the Decline of the American Dream* (Oxford: Oxford University Press, 2008), although he is primarily concerned with insecurity produced by policy changes regarding healthcare, insurance, retirement, and so on.

39. Kathi Weeks, *The Problem with Work: Feminism, Marxism, Antiwork Politics, and Postwork Imaginaries* (Durham, NC: Duke University Press, 2011), 197, 199.

40. Ibid., 198.

41. Hadot, *Philosophy as a Way of Life,* 132.

42. See Athanasius, *The Life of Anthony (and the Letter to Marcellinus),* trans. Robert C. Gregg (Mahwah, NJ: Paulist: 1980), 45 (commenting on 1 Cor. 15:31).

43. Deut. 15:9, following Hadot's translation of the Septuagint passage commented on by Basil; Hadot, *Philosophy as a Way of Life,* 130.

44. See Mullainathan and Shafir, *Scarcity,* chapters 8–10.

45. Compare Hadot, *Philosophy as a Way of Life,* 259–260; he, as usual, is interested in drawing out similarities rather than differences among spiritual practices.

46. See Augustine, *Confessions,* trans. R. S. Pine-Coffin (London: Penguin, 1961), book 11, section 15.

47. See Hadot, *Philosophy as a Way of Life,* 222–228, 268, for a comparison with the way the present is our happiness in Stoicism and Epicureanism.

48. Compare Michel Foucault, *The Hermeneutics of the Subject,* trans. Graham Burchell (New York: Picador, 2005), 132, on Stoic attempts to escape "stultitia."

49. Augustine, *Confessions,* 286, 287 (book 12, sections 9 and 11); see also book 12, section 15.

50. See Søren Kierkegaard, *Christian Discourses Etc.,* trans. Walter Lowrie (Princeton, NJ: Princeton University Press, 1974), 355.

51. Compare Foucault, *Hermeneutics of the Subject,* 133.

5
Another World?

1. For the distinction between present future and future present, see Niklas Luhmann, *Risk: A Sociological Theory*, trans. Rhodes Barrett (New Brunswick, NJ: Aldine Transaction, 2008). For the application of this distinction to financial instruments and markets, see Joseph Vogl, *The Specter of Capital*, trans. Joachim Redner and Robert Savage (Stanford, CA: Stanford University Press, 2015), 111, and, especially, Elena Esposito, *The Future of Futures: The Time of Money in Financing and Society* (Cheltenham, UK: Edward Elgar, 2011).

2. Fredric Jameson, *The Seeds of Time* (New York: Columbia University Press, 1994), xii.

3. Here and in the next several paragraphs I follow the analysis of modernity in terms of the difference between danger and risk found in Luhmann, *Risk*.

4. Vogl, *Specter of Capital*, 111.

5. See the application of Luhmann's account of risk in modernity to finance in Esposito, *Future of Futures*, and Vogl, *Specter of Capital*.

6. Here and in what follows I am influenced by the demand-based understanding of valuation in financial markets found in André Orléan, *The Empire of Value: A New Foundation for Economics*, trans. M. B. DeBevoise (Cambridge: MIT Press, 2014), chapters 6–7.

7. Here and in what follows I am influenced by the analysis of such "black swan" events in Nassim Nicholas Taleb, *The Black Swan: The Impact of the Highly Improbable* (New York: Random House, 2010).

8. See, for example, the discussion of the problem of pricing derivatives in Esposito, *Future of Futures*, 114–115, 136–137.

9. This is one of the major points made in Taleb, *Black Swan*.

10. For criticisms of this idea, see Orléan, *Empire of Value*, 191–196; Esposito, *Future of Futures*, 141–151; and Taleb, *Black Swan*, 245–252.

11. See, for example, the discussion of the October 1987 flash-crash in Taleb, *Black Swan*, 276, and Orléan, *Empire of Value*, 227.

12. See the analogy with the decimation of turkeys at Thanksgiving in Taleb, *Black Swan*, chapter 4. Their dying off at Thanksgiving is a normal, basic feature of this market, even if not predictable from the turkeys' own point of view given their fat and happy lives up to that point.

13. See the stress on consensus as a price-setting mechanism in Orléan, *Empire of Value*, 211–220.

14. See Esposito, *Future of Futures*, 143–144.

15. Ibid., 147–148.

16. See Orléan, *Empire of Value*, 190.

17. This is one of the major points made in Taleb, *Black Swan*.

18. I am following here the development of this point in Esposito, *Future of Futures*.

19. See the treatment of Stoicism in Michel Foucault, *The Hermeneutics of the Subject*, trans. Graham Burchell (New York: Picador, 2005), 321–323, 469–473.

20. For this account of acting with reservations on matters outside of one's control, see Brad Inwood, *Ethics and Human Action in Early Stoicism* (Oxford: Clarendon, 1985), 119–126.

21. I make these comparisons with Stoicism to show, as I did in earlier chapters, its alignment with the present configuration of capitalism, rather than, as Foucault seems to suggest, its possible relevance as a form of counter-practice to it.

22. For a description of many such ways in which future possibility is foreclosed, see Esposito, *Future of Futures*, 72, 83–84, 116, 119–120, 130, 156, 174.

23. See, for example, Gregory of Nyssa's allegorizing of hell, as discussed in Kathryn Tanner, *Christ the Key* (Cambridge: Cambridge University Press, 2010), chapter 2.

24. Søren Kierkegaard, *Christian Discourses Etc.,* trans. Walter Lowrie (Princeton, NJ: Princeton University Press, 1974), 76–77.

25. For this sort of move, see Jürgen Moltmann, *Theology of Hope: On the Ground and the Implications of a Christian Eschatology,* trans. James W. Leitch (New York: Harper and Row, 1975).

26. I am following Walter Benjamin here, according to the account given of his work in Terry Eagleton, *Hope without Optimism* (Charlottesville: University of Virginia Press, 2015), 28–43, and disagreeing with Moltmann's reproach of the epiphanic in *Theology of Hope*.

6

Which World?

1. Juliet B. Schor, *The Overworked American: The Unexpected Decline of Leisure* (New York: Basic Books, 1993), 139.

2. For further discussion of the moralistic attention to individuals characteristic of the old Protestant work ethic, see Kathi Weeks, *The Problem with Work: Feminism, Marxism, Antiwork Politics, and Postwork Imaginaries* (Durham, NC: Duke University Press, 2011), 51–57.

3. See, for example, Frédéric Lordon, *Willing Slaves of Capital: Spinoza and Marx on Desire,* trans. Gabriel Ash (London: Verso, 2014), 118–122, 128–130,

and Luc Boltanski and Eve Chiapello, *The New Spirit of Capitalism,* trans. Gregory Elliott (London: Verso, 2007), 382–384. I do not think these criticisms go far enough (as becomes apparent later), unless they have the effect of undermining the whole idea of individual merit pay.

4. See Paul du Gay, *Consumption and Identity at Work* (London: Sage, 1996), 136, 164.

5. See Daniel Defert, " 'Popular Life' and Insurance Technology," in *The Foucault Effect: Studies in Governmentality,* ed. Graham Burchell, Colin Gordon, and Peter Miller (Chicago: University of Chicago Press, 1991), 212–215, 231–232. He is primarily concerned to show how state provision of welfare is itself a kind of de-socialization of assistance in mutual aid societies. For discussion of the way the need for individual insurance arises with the shift away from social insurance provided by a welfare state, see Pat O'Malley, "Risk and Responsibility," in *Foucault and Political Reason: Liberalism, Neo-Liberalism, and Rationalities of Government,* ed. Andrew Barry, Thomas Osborne, and Nikolas Rose (Chicago: University of Chicago Press, 1996), 189–207.

6. See François Ewald, "Insurance and Risk," in Burchell, Gordon, and Miller, eds., *Foucault Effect,* 204–206.

7. O'Malley, "Risk and Responsibility," 199–202. See also Nikolas Rose, "Governing 'Advanced' Liberal Democracies," in Barry, Osborne, and Rose, eds., *Foucault and Political Reason,* 57–62.

8. O'Malley, "Risk and Responsibility," 203–204.

9. See Anne Gray, *Unsocial Europe: Social Protection or Flexploitation?* (London: Pluto Press, 2004). The character of the shift to workfare in the United States under President Bill Clinton is well known; see, for example, Linda Gordon, *Pitied but Not Entitled: Single Mothers and the History of Welfare* (Cambridge: Harvard University Press, 1995). On the way economic inequality can infiltrate and compromise the rights of citizens, see T. H. Marshall and Tom Bottomore, *Citizenship and Social Class* (London: Pluto Press, 1992).

10. Maurizio Lazzarato, *The Making of Indebted Man: An Essay on the Neoliberal Condition,* trans. Joshua David Jordan (Los Angeles: Semiotext[e], 2012), 101–102, 198–199.

11. See Rose, "Governing 'Advanced' Liberal Democracies," 56–57, and especially O'Malley, "Risk and Responsibility," 189–191. They are both following the basic lines of the argument found in Michel Foucault, *The Birth of Biopolitics,* trans. Graham Burchell (New York: Picador, 2008).

12. See O'Malley, "Risk and Responsibility," 199–202.

13. See Ofer Sharone, "Engineering Overwork: Bell-Curve Management at a High-Tech Firm," in *Fighting for Time: Shifting Boundaries of Work and*

Social Life, ed. Cynthia Fuchs Epstein and Arne L. Kalleberg (New York: Russell Sage, 2004), 193–201.

14. For this metaphor, see once again Nassim Nicholas Taleb, *The Black Swan: The Impact of the Highly Improbable* (New York: Random House, 2010), chapter 4.

15. See, for example, Robert H. Frank and Philip J. Cook, *The Winner-Take-All Society: Why the Few at the Top Get So Much More Than the Rest of Us* (New York: Penguin, 1996).

16. For the meaning of positional goods, see Fred Hirsch, *Social Limits to Growth* (Cambridge: Harvard University Press, 1976), chapter 3. See also the very helpful discussion of Hirsh in William E. Connolly, *Capitalism and Christianity, American Style* (Durham, NC: Duke University Press, 2008), 95–103; I took my example of standing on tiptoe from him, 96–97.

17. See Elena Esposito, *The Future of Futures: The Time of Money in Financing and Society* (Cheltenham, UK: Edward Elgar, 2011), chapter 8.

18. See Karen Ho, *Liquidated: An Ethnography of Wall Street* (Durham, NC: Duke University Press, 2009), 257–271, and David L. Collinson and Margaret Collinson, "The Power of Time: Leadership, Management and Gender," in Epstein and Kalleberg, eds., *Fighting for Time,* 230–231.

19. For this contrast with the liberal state, see Foucault, *Birth of Biopolitics.* See also the account of ordo-liberalism in Pierre Dardot and Christian Laval, *The New Way of the World: On Neoliberal Society,* trans. Gregory Elliott (London: Verso, 2013), chapter 3.

20. The intertwining of competitive and individualistic norms in neoliberalism is one of the major claims made in Dardot and Laval, *New Way of the World.*

21. See Somogy Varga, *Authenticity as an Ethical Ideal* (New York: Routledge, 2012), 134–135. He is discussing here the difference between what he calls expressive and performative authenticity.

22. John Bellamy Foster and Robert W. McChesney, *The Endless Crisis: How Monopoly-Finance Capital Produces Stagnation and Upheaval from the USA to China* (New York: Monthly Review, 2012), 77–84, 112–113.

23. See André Orléan, *The Empire of Value: A New Foundation for Economics,* trans. M. B. DeBevoise (Cambridge: MIT Press, 2014), chapter 2.

24. Ibid., 233–238.

25. See I. I. Rubin, *Essays on Marx's Theory of Value,* trans. Milos Samardzija and Fredy Perlman (Delhi: Aakar Books, 2008), and the discussion of Rubin in Orléan, *Empire of Value,* 30–34. The usual contrast is with a planned economy.

26. See Varga, *Authenticity,* 151, 153.

27. See, inter alia, du Gay, *Consumption and Identity,* 84.

28. See Orléan, *Empire of Value,* 220–226.

29. For the general point about the relatively greater independence of owners of capital in finance-dominated capitalism, see Lordon, *Willing Slaves,* 17–20, 41–48.

30. Defined in Taleb, *Black Swan,* 27.

31. Ibid., 106.

32. See Melvin J. Lerner, *The Belief in a Just World: A Fundamental Delusion* (New York: Plenum Press, 1980).

33. See Ho, *Liquidated,* chapter 1.

34. See P. D. Anthony, *The Ideology of Work* (Abingdon, UK: Routledge, 2001), chapter 1.

35. For more on this contrast of God's grace with private property, see Kathryn Tanner, *Economy of Grace* (Minneapolis: Fortress Press, 2005).

36. See Kathryn Tanner, "Why Are We Here?" in *Why Are We Here? Everyday Questions and the Christian Life,* ed. Ronald F. Thiemann and William C. Placher (Harrisburg, PA: Trinity Press International, 1998), 5–16. Note that God's intentions with respect to the entire world, and not just humans, are similarly non-purposive. Animals are fundamentally created simply to reflect God's glory, too. And that means they are not created merely to be of use in the human project.

37. This is one of the main conclusions in Anthony, *The Ideology of Work.*

38. I am contesting here the solution offered in Lordon, *Willing Slaves.*

39. See Juliet B. Schor, *Plenitude* (New York: Penguin, 2010).

40. This would seem to be what Foucault recommends.

41. Paul Lafargue, *The Right to Be Lazy,* ed. Bernard Marszalek (Chicago: Charles H. Kerr and AK Press, 2011).

42. See Maurizio Lazzarato, *Governing by Debt,* trans. Joshua David Jordan (South Pasadena, CA: Semiotext[e], 2013), 245–255.

43. See, for example, Jean Baudrillard, *The Mirror of Production,* trans. Mark Poster (St. Louis: Telos, 1975). He is following Georges Bataille here.

44. Du Gay, *Consumption and Identity,* 55 (citing Nikolas Rose).

45. I am heavily influenced here by the understanding of Christian community in Friedrich Schleiermacher, *The Christian Faith,* trans. H. R. MacIntosh (Philadelphia: Fortress Press, 1976). I am, however, amending his account in a more objectivist direction, to emphasize the prior universal efficacy of Christ, in ways he might well consider "magical."

46. See Martin Luther, "God or Mammon: How Christians Should Not Be Anxious about Their Food and Raiment," in *The Complete Sermons of Martin Luther,* vol. 3, parts 1–2, ed. and trans. John Nicholas Lenker (Grand Rapids, MI: Baker Books, 2000), 107–110.

47. Cf. Jennifer A. Herdt, "Christian Civility, Courtly Civility, and the Code of the Streets," *Modern Theology* 25, no. 4 (2009): 556–557.

48. See Defert, " 'Popular Life,' " 213, 231–232.

49. See Bruce Lee Webb and Lynne Adele, *As Above, So Below: Art of the American Fraternal Society* (Austin: University of Texas Press, 2015).

50. Jason David BeDuhn, *The Manichaean Body: In Discipline and Ritual* (Baltimore: Johns Hopkins University Press, 2002), 115 (citing Chinese sources); see also 225.

51. Peter Brown, *Through the Eye of a Needle: Wealth, the Fall of Rome, and the Making of Christianity in the West, 350–550 AD* (Princeton, NJ: Princeton University Press, 2012), 165, 166; see also 157–160.

52. Compare the imagery in Baudrillard, *Mirror of Production,* 65–66, 161–163, 164–165, 166.

Index